James Parton

The Danish Islands

Are We Bound in Honor to Pay for Them?

James Parton

The Danish Islands
Are We Bound in Honor to Pay for Them?

ISBN/EAN: 9783744709927

Printed in Europe, USA, Canada, Australia, Japan

Cover: Foto ©Suzi / pixelio.de

More available books at **www.hansebooks.com**

THE DANISH ISLANDS:

ARE WE BOUND IN HONOR TO PAY FOR THEM?

By JAMES PARTON.

BOSTON:
FIELDS, OSGOOD, & CO.,
SUCCESSORS TO TICKNOR AND FIELDS.
1869.

THE DANISH ISLANDS.

THE QUESTION STATED.

THE main question to be here considered is one of simple right or wrong, — Are we morally bound to ratify the treaty with Denmark, and pay the seven millions and a half in gold for the Danish Islands, St. Thomas and St. John?

It does not concern this particular inquiry, whether we want the Islands or not, nor whether the price is excessive or fair, nor whether other and better islands can be had cheaper or for nothing. Something may be said on these points by and by, because it is convenient to have all the facts of the case presented at one view, so that busy people may get at them easily and quickly. But the principal question is, as between the United States and Denmark, *Have we bought the islands?* Must we ratify the treaty and pay the money, or commit a wrong upon a friendly nation, and bring just reproach upon our own good name?

In presenting this subject, my first and principal task is to relate the history of the treaty of cession from the beginning. The reader will then, I think, be in a position to judge how far Mr. Seward's purchase morally binds the United States, and whether we can honorably repudiate the treaty or not.

BEGINNING OF THE NEGOTIATION.

Dinners play an important part in European diplomacy. In Washington, however, I am told, although dining together is, during a great part of the year, the sole amusement of the representatives of foreign powers, serious business is seldom broached on festive occasions. But it is broached sometimes, as the reader is about to discover.

On the seventh of January, 1865, M. de Geoffroy, the Chargé d'Affaires of France, gave a large dinner-party at Washington, which was attended by most of the diplomatic corps, and, among the rest, by General Raasloff, Minister from Denmark. Mr. Seward was also one of the guests. I do not know why it happened, but it did happen, that both the Secretary of State and the Danish Minister arrived at the house of M. de Geoffroy half an hour before dinner was announced, and they found themselves in the drawing-room almost alone. A few days before, when the legations made their New Year's call at the Presidential mansion, Mr. Lincoln had singled out the Danish Minister from the rest, had paid him marked attention, and engaged him for a long time in conversation on indifferent subjects. In a European court this would have meant something, but the circumstance does not appear to have excited the curiosity of the Danish Minister at the time, and he would probably have forgotten it if the events which I am about to relate had not recalled it to his mind. General Raasloff had been a resident of the United States for thirteen years, during which his diplomatic duties had not been arduous, but he had become intimately acquainted with the leading men in Washington, by whom he was held in high esteem for his social and manly qualities. He was one of that very small number among the diplomatic corps resident in Washington, who during the rebellion sympathized with the United States, and believed in the final triumph of freedom and civilization. Neither he nor his country was to be reckoned among our "neutral friends." Mr. Lincoln's familiarity with him, therefore, was not remarkable.

It is safe to conjecture that the early attendance of Mr. Seward and General Raasloff at the dinner-party was not wholly the result of accident. Be that as it may, the Secretary of State took the Danish Minister aside, and conducted him to a sofa in a distant part of the room, upon which they both sat down. Mr. Seward's manner was that of a man who has something to communicate which he hopes will both interest and gratify the person to whom it is addressed. He was cordiality itself, and evidently exerted himself to make the most agreeable impression possible.

The United States, he said, wished to purchase the group of West India Islands belonging to Denmark, provided, of course, the Danish Government should be willing to part with them. We had been compelled by the war, he continued, to become a great maritime power, and hence a good harbor and depot in the West Indies had become a matter of great importance to the United States, if not a necessity. He had thought for years of opening a negotiation for the purchase of those Islands, but a favorable conjuncture had not presented itself until recently. Now, however, that peace was re-established between Denmark and the Great German Powers, the happy moment seemed to have arrived, and he was ready to avail himself of it. To this the Secretary of State added some obliging and agreeable remarks, designed to enlist the favorable regard of the minister with whom he was conversing.

"I feel persuaded," said he, "that, in addressing myself to you, my proposition will be communicated to the Danish Government with the greatest possible delicacy and discretion."

Secrecy, he added, he considered so important that he had refrained from seeking in a public way any preliminary information with regard to the condition and value of the Islands, nor would he try to promote the affair through any other channel or by any other means. It was his intention to preserve the most loyal and the most friendly attitude towards the Danish Government, and he assured the Danish Minister that the negotiations to which he hoped his proposal would lead should be conducted on the part of the United States in *the most generous, chivalrous, and delicate manner*. As a matter of course, he continued, the United States could not wish to see those Islands get into the hands of any other power; but, in making this remark, he said that it was far from his intention to insinuate that the United States did not absolutely recognize the right of the Danish Government to dispose of them. Thus, Mr. Seward.

Abraham Lincoln, the reader will bear in mind, was our President then, and the war had not ended. In making this communication to the Danish Minister, the Secretary of State spoke in the name of President Lincoln, who was certainly of all men the last to scan the map of the world with a view to the purchase of outlying islands. Nevertheless, Mr. Lincoln, after full consideration, had sanctioned the scheme which Mr. Seward now entered upon. The events of the war had brought him to it,— him, a Western man, naturally averse to the acquisition of territory southward, prudent, slow to take the initiative, and keenly sensible of the value of the millions which those Islands would cost.

I have said that events had brought him to it. I should perhaps have said, rather, *an event*, — the concession of belligerent rights to the Confederates by Great Britain, together with the active, ruthless hostility of the greatest naval power of the world to the United States when its existence was at stake. During the war, I am informed, on the best living authority, there were British coaling-stations off our coast, from which British merchants were enabled to supply the Confederate cruisers and blockade-runners with coal. Mr. Welles sent vessels to the English waters for the supply of the national ships of the United States, but the public opinion of England supported the British Government in ordering them away. At the Western Islands, at the Azores, at Madeira, our ships were refused coal and supplies through the influence of Great Britain. Finally, we established a coal-yard at St. Thomas, one of the three Danish Islands concerning which Mr. Seward and General Raasloff conversed on the sofa at the French Legation.

He selected this particular island for two reasons : 1. It is the central and commanding position of the West Indies ; and, 2. It belonged to a power which had shown, throughout the war, that friendly partiality for the United States which became a civilized and humane nation. The Rebel flag never floated in a Danish port. The Danish Governor of St. Thomas, though he was compelled to enforce the regulations of a neutral harbor, granted all the favors to Admiral Wilkes and his successors which an official person can grant when his heart prompts him. The Admiral, for example, was accustomed to evade the twenty-four-hour rule by keeping a vessel just outside, and letting her loose upon any blockade-runner that ventured to leave.

The Governor's post was no sinecure during the war. The ships of both flags were so ravenous for coal that he was in continual fear of armed vessels making a seizure of the precious deposit, and he was obliged to station troops to defend the coal-yards. Extreme inconvenience was also experienced by our admirals commanding on that station from their being obliged to send prizes fifteen hundred miles to be adjudicated, and damaged steamers fifteen hundred miles for repairs.

It was, however, the immense importance of having a coaling-station of *our own* in the West Indies that decided Mr. Lincoln, and caused him to give his full and hearty consent to Mr. Seward's opening a negotiation for the purchase of the Danish Islands. He may be said to have begun the negotiation himself on the second of January, 1865, when he smiled benignantly upon, and chatted familiarly with, the representative of his Danish Majesty, in the Blue Room of the White House.

Mr. Seward's proposition took the Danish Minister completely by surprise.

"The inhabitants of the Islands," he said, at length, "are happy and contented under Danish rule."

"I cheerfully admit that," replied Mr. Seward, "but I cannot help thinking that annexation to the United States would bring with it sufficient advantage to render the inhabitants favorable to the transfer."

Mr. Seward continued the conversation for some minutes longer, repeatedly urging upon the Danish Minister the necessity of treating the affair as a profound secret, to be disclosed only to those who must necessarily be informed of it. England, France, and Spain, he thought, would object to a cession of the Islands to the United States, and might endeavor to defeat it by diplomatic arts, if the proposal should be made public.

"I decline beforehand," said he, "to be responsible for any divulgence which may possibly occur, as it certainly will not come from me; and I determined to make this overture through you, General, because your reserve is well known to me."

Mr. Seward paused. The company were all assembled. The dinner was more than ready. But the master of the house deferred the opening of the dining-room doors, as if aware that something interesting was going forward on that distant sofa. General Raasloff, observing that Mr. Seward had completely expressed himself, quietly said, "I do not think his Majesty's Government will be inclined to part with our West India possessions, but I will communicate your proposition."

He would have said more, for the scheme was repugnant to him as a Danish citizen; but he remembered that he was a Danish diplomatist also, and felt it to be his duty to leave his government untrammelled by any expressions of his own for or against the project. Dinner was announced; the conference broke up; and the distinguished party streamed into the dining-room.

The Danish Minister lost no time in giving a full account to his government of this interesting interview. In the course of his despatch, dated January 9, 1865, he spoke much of the warmth and cordiality of Mr. Seward's manner.

"Our conversation," he wrote, "left no doubt in my mind as to the lively desire on the part of the Government of the United States that their proposition should be well received by us, nor as to the delicacy and liberality with which it is their intention eventually to treat that matter. . . . . It is extremely painful for me to think that, after having recently lost so much territory, we should now be driven to part also with our West India possessions, bound to our country by so many ties."

THE NEGOTIATION INTERRUPTED.

Events, some of which were glorious and others most bloody and terrible, retarded the negotiation.

For several weeks nothing more occurred in it, except that on the fourth of February, the day on which Mr. Seward returned from the celebrated Peace Conference with Confederate leaders at Fortress Monroe, he met the Danish Minister, and told him that he adhered to the proposition which he had made on the seventh of January. He also said to him that he had neither spoken nor written to any one upon the subject except the President. He probably meant to intimate that the close of the war, which then seemed imminent, would not alter the intentions of the government with regard to the purchase of the Islands.

A month later, Mr. Seward was thrown from his carriage, and so severely injured that he was confined to his bed. A week after the accident, the Danish Minister called at the State Department to say that he had received an answer from his government with regard to the proposed purchase. That answer, I may observe in passing, was not a point-blank refusal to sell, but as near to that as so polite and cautious a people as the Danes could be expected to make. At first, the project of transferring the Islands to the United States had not one friend in Denmark. General Raasloff, the Danish Minister, was not favorable to it; the conservative party opposed it, to a man; the benevolent King, warmly attached to his subjects, could not bear the thought of parting with any more of them. The Kingdom had just lost two provinces, which comprised a third of its territory and two fifths of its population, and the people felt disheartened and humiliated. When the project was whispered about among them at length, the general exclamation was,— "Have we not lost territory enough? Must we part with more of our possessions? Must our colonies go too?"

Nor was there any reason in the financial condition of the country why the Islands should be sold; for, even after such heavy misfortunes, honest Denmark had an income equal to her expenditure, and her five-per cent bonds ranged, as they now do, above par. The sentiment of dominion, the pride of a mother country in her colonies, the strong attachment to possessions which Denmark had held for nearly two hundred years, — all such feelings, intensified by recent calamity, were against the transfer.

When the Danish Minister called at the State Department to communicate the reply of his government, he was received by Mr. Frederick Seward, the Assistant Secretary of State, who was not in the secret. The Minister could therefore only charge him with a message to his father, to the effect that a communication from the Danish Government had been received. It was on the twelfth of April, 1865, that this message was delivered.

Two days after occurred the assassination of Mr. Lincoln, and the attempt to assassinate the Secretary of State. Mr. Frederick Seward was also prostrated by a murderous stroke, and the whole machinery of government seemed for a time suspended.

Nowhere in the world was the news of these tragic events received with profounder horror and more genuine sympathy than in Denmark. The King hastened to express his grief to the American Minister, whose house was continually filled with the most distinguished people in Copenhagen, who came to express their sympathy. Nevertheless, the feelings of the court and ministry with regard to the cession of the Islands remained unchanged, and the Danish Minister was expressly ordered *not to initiate a renewal of the subject*, either with Mr. Seward, or, if he should die, with his successor. And so the matter rested for many weeks.

CHANGE IN THE DANISH MINISTRY. — GENERAL RAASLOFF AND MR. SEWARD AGAIN CONVERSE.

It was not until near the close of August, 1865, that social intercourse was renewed between the Secretary of State and the Minister from Denmark. When at last they did meet, the proposed purchase of the Islands was not mentioned by either of them. They were together many times during the latter half of the year 1865, but on no occasion was the subject alluded to between them until the twenty-ninth of December, when the Danish Minister called upon the Secretary of State to impart to him the substance of new instructions just received from Copenhagen. A new Ministry, it seems, had come into power in Denmark, who were not so decidedly opposed to the sale of the Islands as the Ministry just retired. Accordingly, General Raasloff had now to inform Mr. Seward that his government was not absolutely opposed to the sale of the Islands, but that there were weighty reasons against the sale, and that, therefore, the Danish Government could not take the proposal into consideration unless they knew how large a sum the United States were prepared to give. Their decision, in fact, would depend in a great measure upon the liberality of the offer which the United States might make.

The Secretary of State, still feeble in health, and intending to start on the following day for a month's cruise among the West India Islands, said that he did not know whether the present was a favorable moment for such a negotiation, and that he must ask for time to consider it.

General Raasloff replied that there was no need of haste; he was not pressed for an answer; and he had only called then because he thought the Secretary ought to know the present disposition of the Danish Government.

Mr. Seward remarked in reply that, when they had first conversed on the subject, Mr. Lincoln was President, but that now the affair would have to be conducted under the direction of President Johnson, who, however, was not unfavorable to the purchase. He added that, as he was to leave Washington the next day for the recovery of his health, he should have no opportunity of conversing with the President before his return. He intended to visit Havana, and perhaps St. Thomas, but his visit to the island last named would have no connection whatever with the proposed purchase. Again the Secretary of State enjoined secrecy, to the necessity of which the Danish Minister assented.

Mr. Seward sailed in the De Soto on the last day of the year 1865. He visited the Danish Islands; and although, so far as I can ascertain, the secret of the preliminary negotiation had been faithfully kept by those to whom it was necessarily intrusted, yet it seems as if the whole world considered Mr. Seward's visit to St. Thomas in the light of an inspection previous to purchase. So the people of the Islands regarded it, and so the press of the United States interpreted it. Earl Russell, then at the head of Foreign Affairs in England, conversed upon Mr. Seward's visit with the Danish Minister in London, who, not being in the secret, could not enlighten his Lordship, but promised him that nothing should be done towards selling the Islands to the United States without the British Government being informed. This promise proved afterwards to be a serious embarrassment to the negotiation, which was only removed by the Danish Government refusing to be bound by an engagement which was totally unauthorized.

It seems to me that here is a striking illustration of the futility of secret diplomacy. Strictly speaking, perhaps, there is no such thing as secret diplomacy; but there is often secrecy enough to do mischief. It is only *secret* diplomacy which could have opposed the cession of these Islands to the United States, because no reason can be given against such a cession which a foreign power would choose to put into print.

Whatever Mr. Seward's intentions may have been in visiting the Danish Islands, it is certain that he was extremely pleased with them, and that his visit greatly quickened his desire to possess them. Returning to Washington on the twenty-eighth of January, 1866, he was closeted on the very next day at the State Department with the Danish Minister. Then it was that the negotiation began in earnest. Mr. Seward asked General Raasloff to repeat the communication which he had made at their last interview, and, when that was done, he said that he was now ready to lay the matter before the President and the Cabinet. He added that he should study the precedents established in the purchase of Louisiana and Florida, with a view of finding a proper basis for the negotiation.

There was then some preliminary skirmishing, as is usual in such cases, with regard to price, each of the gentlemen being desirous to know the ideas of the other on this interesting point. Mr. Seward first asked the Danish Minister whether he knew what his government expected for the Islands. The Minister did not. The Secretary then asked him what price he had himself thought of as reasonable. To this General Raasloff replied that twenty-five millions of dollars seemed to him a reasonable price; at least he could say with certainty that his government would not be willing to negotiate for the transfer unless the United States offered something handsome.

"If my opinion should be asked," added General Raasloff, "which is not probable, I should propose twenty millions as the absolutely minimum price."

During the next six months, while the cession of the Islands was the frequent theme of remark in the newspapers (no newspaper opposing it), the Secretary of State and the Danish Minister conversed often and earnestly on the subject, each endeavoring to get from the other something like a distinct offer. Mr. Seward urged that the usual course was for the seller to name a price, and for the buyer to consider whether he could afford to pay it. General Raasloff could not deny this, but called Mr. Seward's attention to the circumstances which in this instance seemed to justify a reversal of the usual order. Denmark, he observed, was not yet negotiating to cede her Islands. She was endeavoring to ascertain whether the advantages which the United States would offer could equal the certain loss and damage involved in parting with the Islands to the United States. She wanted to know whether or not it was worth while to take the matter into consideration. She did not want to sell; the United States did want to buy. The cession of the Islands to the United States could not but be disagreeable to France and offensive to England,— powers which such a kingdom as Denmark could not wantonly displease nor safely offend. The preliminary question for Denmark was: Will the United States give us money *enough* to compensate us for the injury which the cession of the Islands will certainly do us,— the loss of prestige, the loss of property, the weakening of ties which bind us in alliance with powerful neighbors?

Denmark had, as all nations have, and as all individuals have, objects, desires, dreams, which the possession of a certain sum of money would enable her, as she hoped, to realize. It was, therefore, essential to her, as a preliminary, to have some idea of the amount of pecuniary advantage which she would derive from a transfer of her West India possessions.

A PRICE OFFERED.

Mr. Seward and General Raasloff had many conversations upon this point before either of them showed any signs of yielding. At length, however, when the Danish Minister announced his intention of returning home, and expressed a strong desire to convey to his government a definite proposition, Mr. Seward relented so far as to agree to lay General Raasloff's arguments before the President and the Cabinet, and see if he could obtain their consent to the naming of a price. He did so, but their consent was withheld.

When the Secretary of State communicated to the Danish Minister the continued reluctance of the President and the Cabinet to sanction an offer, he dwelt upon the great necessity there was for all the proceedings in an affair of this nature to be strictly regular and correct. I presume Mr. Seward foresaw the collision between the Executive and Congress, and was exceedingly cautious not to give the Senate any pretext to reject the treaty, nor the House any reason to refuse the money. Mr. Seward said to General Raasloff, in one of their last conversations (June 28, 1866), that "*the Executive could always count upon the assistance of Congress in matters of this kind, provided the proceedings had been correct.*" This remark sank deeply into the mind of the Danish Minister, and it had, at a later stage of the negotiations, a very important, if not a decisive, effect in determining the Danish Government to give its assent to the treaty of cession.

The Government of the United States at length handsomely yielded the point to the Danish Minister, and made him a definite offer. On the seventeenth of July, 1866, shortly before the departure of the Danish Minister for Europe, Mr. Seward requested his attendance at the Department of State. General Raasloff attended accordingly, and, as soon as he was seated, Mr. Seward sent for his son, Mr. Frederick Seward, who brought in the draft of a letter. This letter the Secretary of State read to the Danish Minister, then signed it, and handed it to him. It was as follows: —

["Confidential."]

"DEPARTMENT OF STATE, *Washington, July* 17, 1866.

"SIR, — I have the honor to propose to you that the United States will negotiate with the King of Denmark for the purchase of the Danish Islands in the West Indies, namely, St. Thomas and the adjacent islets Santa Cruz and St. John.

"The United States would be willing to pay for the same five millions of dollars in gold, payable in this country. Negotiation to be made by treaty, which, you will of course understand, will require the constitutional ratification of the Senate.

"Insomuch as you propose to visit Copenhagen, the United States Minister at that place will be instructed to converse with you or with your government on the subject; but should your government conclude to negotiate, the proceedings will be expected to be conducted here, and not elsewhere.

"Accept, sir, the renewed assurance of my high consideration.

"WILLIAM H. SEWARD.

"His Excellency GENERAL RAASLOFF, &c., &c."

In the course of conversation, Mr. Seward remarked that the representative of the United States in Denmark, who would for a time have charge of the affair, would be instructed to take no steps with regard to it before General Raasloff should have arrived at Copenhagen. Mr. Seward further observed that *he was not pressed for an answer* to his offer, and that he should leave it entirely with the Danish Government to negotiate how and when they thought proper.

General Raasloff left the country a few days after. He left us before the hostility between the President and Congress had assumed that aggravated character which it did toward the close of the year 1866. Soon after his arrival at Copenhagen, he was appointed Minister of War, and he was at once so immersed in the great work of reorganizing the Danish Army that he could bestow little attention upon affairs in America.

THE NEGOTIATION TRANSFERRED TO COPENHAGEN.

The American Minister resident at Copenhagen was Mr. George H. Yeaman, of Kentucky, formerly a member of Congress, a very worthy, capable, and patriotic gentleman, who had rendered valuable service to his country in procuring assent to that amendment of the Constitution which annihilated slavery in the United States. On the very day (July 17, 1866) on which Mr. Seward handed his written offer of five millions to General Raasloff, he despatched a copy of the same to Mr. Yeaman, observing to him that he thought it possible that the Danish Government might wish to confer with him upon the subject. Mr. Seward added these words: "Except in this contingency, you are instructed not to allude to the matter, which, under all circumstances, is to be kept strictly confidential."

Count Frijs, the Danish Minister for Foreign Affairs, upon whom, of course, now devolved the care of this negotiation, is a gentleman of great wealth, ancient lineage, and truly elevated character, an honor to the nobility of the Kingdom. Like all of his order, he was originally averse to the cession of the Islands; but, by reflecting upon the subject, he, as well as General Raasloff, had become convinced that the true policy of his country was to part with possessions which, in the event of war, always endangered the neutrality of Denmark without securing to her any equivalent advantage. This opinion he impressed upon the King and the Cabinet, and thus by slow degrees the government was brought to regard the proposition with some degree of favor. Nevertheless, all the latter half of the year 1866 passed away, and the affair had made no sensible progress. The matter had, however, been mentioned by the Danish Ministry to Mr. Yeaman, and some desultory conversation between them on the subject had occurred.

MR. SEWARD BECOMES IMPATIENT OF THE DELAY.

Late in the evening of Saturday, January 19, 1867, Mr. Yeaman received from Mr. Seward, through the London Legation, the following cable despatch: "*Tell Raasloff haste important.*"

The reason why the Secretary of State sent this message was, I believe, that his son, Mr. Frederick Seward, was then on the point of sailing to St. Domingo, where he was to make inquiries with a view to the purchase or lease of the Bay of Samana, in case the harbor of St. Thomas could not be obtained. Mr. Yeaman immediately called upon General Raasloff, and delivered Mr. Seward's message. The General replied, that he had been extremely busy of late, and would be for some time to come, but that he would give the matter his attention. Mr. Yeaman inquired if he thought the affair was making progress. General Raasloff thought it was, but observed that Count Frijs was very cautious and prudent in such things, and felt some hesitation about taking a decisive step. Mr. Yeaman asked if there were any impediments unknown to him, — any except the "hesitation" felt in the Danish Cabinet. General Raasloff said that there was a difficulty at Washington which had occurred to him, — Congress would adjourn before the treaty could be concluded, and therefore it could not be ratified. To this Mr. Yeaman replied, that the President, if necessary, could request the Senate to remain a short time, which had often been done.

"But," said General Raasloff, "there will be no House to appropriate the money."

Mr. Yeaman's reply to this objection shall here be given in his own words, as contained in his despatch to Mr. Seward of the following day.

"*I answered,*" wrote Mr. Yeaman, "*I thought there could*

not possibly be any difficulty about that, as Congress would assuredly not refuse the necessary appropriation to execute the treaty."

Mr. Yeaman added, that he had not the least means of judging whether the Danish Government was dallying with a view of getting a better offer, or whether the delay was owing merely to a general reluctance to sell.

CAUSE OF THE HESITATION IN THE DANISH CABINET, AND HOW THEIR RELUCTANCE WAS OVERCOME.

I can throw some light upon the delay at Copenhagen. There was, indeed, a genuine, general, and profound reluctance to sell the Islands; but this, as just remarked, had been in some degree overcome. But now there was a new cause for distrust and alarm. The President's "swing round the circle" had occurred; the breach between the Executive and Congress seemed past healing; and a natural doubt arose in the minds of prudent Danes, whether Congress would not avail themselves of an opportunity to annoy the Executive by refusing to ratify and execute a treaty. Denmark, unfortunately, had no representative at the time in Washington, and the Danish Ministry were compelled to depend upon the newspapers and Mr. Yeaman for their knowledge of public events and the feelings of the American people. Several circumstances contributed to lull their apprehensions to sleep, and to make them think that Mr. Seward, in his darling policy of annexation, was but executing the will of the people whose servant he was. Those circumstances were the following:—

· 1. In all the discussions to which the rumors respecting the purchase of St. Thomas and St. John had given rise, no voice was heard opposing the purchase. During the heated elections of the fall of 1866, although Mr. Seward had already announced his general policy of annexation, particularly at Raleigh, the year before, yet that policy was never publicly called in question.

2. Mr. Seward's foreign policy seemed to have (and had) the emphatic approval of Mr. Thaddeus Stevens, the leader of that portion of the Republican party which was most opposed to the "man at the other end of the avenue." It so happened that a scene occurred in the House of Representatives, December 13, 1866, which went far towards convincing the Danish Ministry, and quite convinced General Raasloff, that, on all matters of foreign policy, Mr. Stevens and his radical friends were in accord with the Secretary of State, and were entirely disposed to comply with his desires. Mr. Seward had asked the House for what is sometimes called a "blind appropriation" of two hundred and fifty thousand dollars. That is to say, he asked Congress to intrust him with the expenditure of that sum for purposes vaguely described in the appropriation bill as "The contingent expenses of foreign intercourse." Mr. Scofield, of Pennsylvania, an inveterate economist, moved to strike out this item, and supported his motion by some humorous remarks, in which he intimated that it would be cheaper to send Surratt's pardon to him in Europe than to go to the expense of bringing him home, trying him, and *then* pardoning him.

"Before we make this appropriation," said Mr. Scofield, "we should have some explanation of it."

It was Mr. Thaddeus Stevens, Chairman of the Foreign Committee, who made the explanation.

"When this appropriation," said the great radical chief, "was requested by the Secretary of State, it being a larger amount than that department ever asked for before, — and I will say here that the committee have always agreed that the State Department had been managed throughout more economically than any other department of the government, — I did not feel disposed to recommend it, either to the committee or to the House, without knowing the reason for it. Not being very well, I requested the Secretary of State, he being a young man (laughter), to call and explain it to me, which he did with great courtesy. And I may as well say to the gentlemen now, for they may want to know, that we did not talk about anything except this appropriation. (Laughter.) He convinced me, not only that this sum was wanted for useful purposes, *but that it would finally be found to be too small.*"

In the course of his remarks, Mr. Stevens said : " I feel it due to the administration of the State Department to go as far as may be prudent in voting the appropriations asked for it; and however I may differ politically with the head of that department, I cannot allow myself to be influenced by such considerations in acting upon a question of this kind."

The scene concluded thus : —

Mr. Scofield. " The explanation of my colleague is, in general, satisfactory, but he says that there are some 'other items'; and, knowing his partiality toward the administration and his recent intimacy with it, I do not know but that among those 'other items' may be one to pay the expenses of 'swinging round the circle.' If the gentleman will assure us that there is nothing of that kind among the reserved items, I will withdraw my motion."

Mr. Stevens. " I assure the gentleman that there is nothing of that kind included in this appropriation. There are two or three unpaid bills of that account (laughter), but it is expressly understood that they shall not come out of this appropriation."

Mr. Scofield. " Then I withdraw my motion."

The money was then voted. It was known at the time to many members of Congress, and erelong to the public, that a portion of this money was to be used in the acquisition of a West India harbor; and some of it, it is believed, was actually taken by Mr. Frederick Seward to St. Domingo for the purpose. Now, what inference could the Danish Ministry draw from a scene like this, but that the influence of Mr. Seward, as Foreign Secretary, was undiminished in Congress, and that the men most opposed to him in general politics could be most relied on to support his foreign policy ?

3. But all this was nothing in its effect upon the Danish mind compared with the promptitude with which the Alaska treaty was concluded and ratified, together with the arguments adduced in the Senate for the *principle* involved in its ratification.

Seldom has anything of equal importance been done with more business-like despatch than the purchase of Alaska, when once the matter was fairly on the carpet. Passing by the desultory negotiations of former years, the history of the cession can be given in a few lines. In 1866, the fishermen and lumbermen of Washington Territory called the attention of Mr. Seward to the subject, and he conversed upon it with the representative of Russia, renewing previous offers. Baron Stoeckl, being at home on leave late in that year, suggested one day, in conversation with the Grand-Duke Constantine, the solution of the difficulty between the fishermen and lumbermen of both nations by selling out all the Russian possessions in North America to the United States. The Grand-Duke approving the scheme, Baron Stoeckl submitted it to the Emperor, who also approved it. On the return of the Baron to Washington, he at once made known to Mr. Seward the willingness of his government to sell. Only two notes, and those very brief, passed between Baron Stoeckl and Mr. Seward on the subject. March 23, 1867, the Secretary of State made his final offer of seven million two hundred thousand dollars. It was telegraphed to St. Petersburg, and, just six days after, Baron Stoeckl announced to Mr. Seward that the Emperor accepted the offer, and had given him full powers to conclude and sign. On the very next day, March 29, 1867, the Secretary of State and the Russian Minister signed the treaty. June 20th the treaty was ratified by the Senate, and on the eighteenth of October the territory was transferred.

Now the Danish Government not only witnessed this eagerness and promptitude, but they also read the arguments adduced by Mr. Sumner in favor of the ratification of the treaty by the Senate, — arguments which they justly felt would apply with far greater force to a treaty with a power invested with the sanctity of weakness, and one from which a treaty had been urgently *solicited*.

"Now that the treaty," said Mr. Sumner, in his celebrated speech on the Alaska purchase, " has been signed by plenipotentiaries on each side duly empowered, it is difficult to see how we can refuse to complete the purchase without putting to hazard the friendly relations which happily exist between the United States and Russia. *The overtures originally proceeded from us.* After a delay of years, and other intervening propositions, the bargain was at length concluded. It is with nations as with individuals. A bargain once made must be kept. Even if still open to consideration, it must not be lightly abandoned. I am satisfied that the dishonor of this treaty, after what has passed, would be a serious responsibility for our country. As an international question, it would be tried by the public opinion of the world, and there are many who, not appreciating the requirement of our Constitution by which a treaty must have " the advice and consent of the Senate," would regard its rejection as bad faith. There would be jeers at us, and jeers at Russia also; at us for levity in making overtures, and at Russia for levity in yielding to them."

Every word of this applies to the Danish treaty. What could Count Frijs, General Raasloff, and the people of Denmark, think when they read such words as these, except that the chairman of the Senate Committee on Foreign Relations, an illustrious orator and statesman, recognized the *obligation* resting upon Congress to ratify and execute a proper and just treaty made in all the forms by the Executive of the United States with the Executive of another nation? Mr. Sumner confessed, on this occasion, that the *system* of secret purchase was wrong. We all feel it to be so. But honest and respectable little Denmark is not responsible for the system, and ought not to suffer the penalty of our voluntary adherence to it.

Alaska, then, which is now the real obstacle to the acceptance of Mr. Seward's bargain for the Danish Islands, was the chief cause of inducing in the Danish Government a conviction that the people of the United States wanted their Islands, and would willingly pay for them when the treaty had been regularly concluded.

BUT THE NEGOTIATION STILL LINGERS.

"Tell Raasloff haste important," telegraphed Mr. Seward to Mr. Yeaman, on the twelfth of January, 1867; and Mr. Yeaman, as we have seen, conveyed the message to General Raasloff. Yet two months more elapsed before anything further was done. Up to this time, in fact, Denmark had done nothing but politely receive Mr. Seward's offer of five millions. The Danish Government had neither accepted nor declined that offer, neither consented nor refused to negotiate. The affair simply remained in March, 1867, just where it did on the seventeenth of July, 1866, when Mr. Seward handed to General Raasloff the note offering five millions in gold.

After waiting two months, the Secretary of State again telegraphed to Mr. Yeaman: "Want yea or nay now. We can read Danish politicians here as well as Danish politicians can read American in Copenhagen."

The American Minister at once repaired to General Raasloff, and asked him what progress had been made in the affair of the Islands since their last conversation two months before.

"None material," replied General Raasloff. "Count Frijs intends to do it, but does not feel quite ready yet. There is a desire to await the further development of some events in Europe."

"What?" asked Mr. Yeaman.

To this point-blank question, the Danish Minister of War made no particular reply. Mr. Yeaman then said that the Government of the United States would like a more definite answer than General Raasloff had given him reason to expect. The Danish Minister replied: "Something more definite and positive is wanted from the other side, — from your government."

Mr. Yeaman observed that he thought Mr. Seward's offer of five millions was quite explicit, and could hardly be more so. Upon this General Raasloff remarked that he regarded that offer as merely formal, and that it was so regarded at the time.

Those terms, he added, were out of the question, and this Mr. Seward very well understood, and if Mr. Seward would indicate what sum might be expected, the affair could be more promptly concluded. Upon Mr. Yeaman's expressing surprise at this remark, General Raasloff explained: —

"Mr. Seward's note was only intended to open negotiations, and not to fix the price. There are objections and difficulties to be overcome here. It is an unpleasant thing, and the price received would have a good deal to do in overcoming objections and diminishing the unpleasantness of the transaction. Some of the Cabinet are willing to sell, and others are not; but even with those who are willing the smallness of the price offered is an objection to opening negotiations, as they fear it will be construed as an implied willingness to accept something like the sum offered."

Mr. Yeaman then communicated the main sentence of Mr. Seward's yea and nay despatch. Upon receiving which, General Raasloff said he was just going to a Cabinet meeting, and he would communicate the message.

Two months more elapsed, during which Mr. Seward and Mr. Yeaman both urged despatch, and yet no communication was received from the Danish Government. When Mr. Yeaman called the attention of General Raasloff to the matter, that gentleman could only converse upon the subject in general terms, and hold out the hope that erelong his government would propose something positive. There was apprehension, he said, of giving offence to England and France.

I may here mention, also, that there were two other causes of this unfortunate delay. 1. The Danish Cabinet was in imminent danger of defeat upon their military measures in the Danish Parliament, which would have compelled them to resign their places. In that case they would probably have been succeeded by ministers wholly opposed to the cession. 2. There was serious apprehension of war between France and Prussia; and this peril, so near to Denmark, complicated the affair of the cession of the Islands to a degree which I need not here explain.

It was not because Denmark was indifferent to the matter that she hesitated so long, but because the objections to the sale were numerous and weighty, and because the smaller powers of Europe must necessarily conduct their foreign relations with extreme caution. They must beware of giving causes of offence. They must refrain from giving *pretexts* for offence. If the reader will but look upon the map of Europe, and notice the situation of Denmark, and mark how it is at once isolated from and surrounded by mighty nations,— Russia, Prussia, England, France, to say nothing of its kindred states on the other side of the channel, — if the reader, I say, will observe the situation of Denmark, both geographical and moral, he will be at no loss to comprehend why, in a matter of so much moment, Count Frijs should have paused long before taking an irretrievable step.

THE NEGOTIATION QUICKENS ITS PACE.

At length, on the seventeenth of May, 1867, Mr. Yeaman received a note from General Raasloff, informing him that Count Frijs wished to see him that evening. At the time appointed he attended at the residence of Count Frijs, where the Count, General Raasloff, and himself conferred on the subject of the cession.

Count Frijs began the conference by saying that Mr. Seward's offer of five millions had been duly considered, and was declined; but the government had concluded to comply with Mr. Seward's evident desire, and make a counter proposition. They would cede, he continued, the group of three islands for fifteen millions of dollars; or they would sell the two islands of St. Thomas and St. John for ten millions, with the option of taking Santa Cruz for five millions more. Count Frijs explained, that the ratification of the treaty of cession by the Rigsdag would be necessary, and that the Danish Government would require that the consent of the people of the Islands should be freely and formally given. He also recommended that the negotiation should be conducted at Copenhagen, because in that case the treaty could be ratified without delay.

In ten days, by the assistance of the cable, Mr. Yeaman was in receipt of Mr. Seward's answer to this proposition, which was in substance this: The United States will pay for the three islands seven millions and a half in gold.

Mr. Seward objected, however, to accepting as a condition the consent of the people of the Islands, and thought it sufficient if they had the free choice to return to Denmark within two years, or to remain and become American citizens. The Secretary of State consented that the negotiation should be conducted at Copenhagen, and sent Mr. Yeaman a draft of such a treaty as he would accept, and a full power to conclude and sign.

Mr. Yeaman lost no time in communicating these instructions to the Danish Minister for Foreign Affairs, who promised that he should have an early answer. Mr. Yeaman met General Raasloff on the same day, who also said that the answer would be promptly returned, and gave it as his distinct but unofficial opinion that that answer would be NO. Some days after General Raasloff intimated unofficially, but "very distinctly," that the offer of seven millions and a half would not be accepted, but that there was another sum which he thought would certainly be, and that was eleven millions and a quarter,— that is, seven millions and a half for St. Thomas and St. John, and one half of that sum for Santa Cruz.

Nearly a month passed before Mr. Yeaman was summoned by Count Frijs to receive an official reply to Mr. Seward's offer. He was sent for at length, however, and the reply was precisely such as General Raasloff had predicted, namely, seven millions and a half for the two islands, and the privilege of taking the third for three millions and three quarters. This odd sum of eleven and a quarter millions was fixed upon by the Danish Ministers because it represents twenty millions of Danish rix-dollars, which was the smallest amount they then deemed it safe to propose to the Rigsdag as the price of the three islands.

With regard to taking a vote of the people of the Islands before the cession, Count Frijs declared that this was a condition absolutely indispensable. Besides being right in itself, and the established custom of Europe, the government of Denmark was committed to the principle by the treaty of Prague, which retroceded to Denmark the northern districts of the Duchy of Schleswig, provided they should, by means of a free vote, express a wish to remain a part of that Kingdom. Denmark, added Count Frijs, was just then intensely interested in the result of the impending vote, and would in no case, and for no consideration, consent to a transfer of the Islands until their inhabitants had given their free consent to it.

Mr. Seward's second offer being thus formally rejected by the Danish Government, Mr. Yeaman now informed Count Frijs that his instructions obliged him to announce that the offer of the United States was withdrawn, and the negotiation ended. He then formally withdrew the offer, and the negotiation was suspended.

In descanting upon this result in a private letter to the Secretary of State, Mr. Yeaman ventured an opinion that seven and a half millions was cheap for the two Islands, and suggested that it would be sound policy in the United States to acquire St. Thomas and St. John at that price, and leave Santa Cruz for future consideration. In the course of this letter, he made a remark or two which throws light upon the feeling of Denmark at the time.

"I find the gentlemen of this government," he wrote, "a little sensitive upon all questions of dignity, prestige, and equality. This is natural. They feel weak and in some degree abandoned by one or two allies, and, no doubt, are more exacting now in the formal part of diplomatic intercourse than they once would have been. I am impressed that a hearty, friendly, somewhat imposing visit of the navy in considerable force would make a good impression. They are in a condition to appreciate attention and sympathy. If General Sherman makes his trip (to the East), tell him to call here and spend a while."

THE NEGOTIATION RESUMED.

Nearly another month of delay. July 6, 1867, Mr. Seward telegraphed to Mr. Adams in London: "Tell Yeaman close with Denmark's offer. St. John, St. Thomas, seven and a half millions. Report brief quick by cable. Send treaty ratified immediately."

Mr. Yeaman at once sought an interview with the Danish ministers for the purpose of making known to them these new instructions, but did not obtain it at once. "One cannot easily hasten affairs of any sort in Denmark," wrote Mr. Yeaman. "In everything, from cobbler to king, they are the most deliberate and leisurely people in the world."

A few days passed. When next the American Minister met Count Frijs and General Raasloff, Mr. Seward's terms were accepted by them, and only one obstacle remained to the immediate signing of the treaty. Denmark still refused to transfer the Islands unless with the consent of the inhabitants. Mr. Seward still objected to that. It is painful to an American citizen to see the representative of the Republic opposing a measure so just, so reasonable, and in such perfect harmony with American principles. It is, however, but fair that the reader should know the reasons for this opposition, as given by Mr. Yeaman. In relating this important and nearly decisive interview, he wrote:—

"I have lost no opportunity to impress upon them, in the most earnest and explicit manner, the very great preference of myself and my government that the cession shall be absolute, and not subject to any further conditions; and that it cannot be in accordance with the feelings of either government that *the matter should fail after a treaty had been signed*, and that nothing should be done that would invite or present an opportunity for the influence and counter influence in the Islands of those three great Powers which would much rather see the matter fail than succeed."

The Danish Ministry, however, were immovable. It was a

point which they *could* not concede, nor would the Rigsdag have ratified the treaty if they had. Mr. Yeaman, therefore, who was disposed to yield if the treaty could not be had without, asked for further instructions.

"Do not agree to submit question," replied Mr. Seward by cable, July 20, 1867; "Congress soon adjourns."

Here again was a dead lock, which the Danish Ministry, intensely preoccupied with its own affairs, were in no haste to undo. Mr. Seward, weary of the delay, wrote to Mr. Yeaman soon after: "You are authorized to say that, in the opinion of this department, promptness in the pending negotiation is essential to its success and the acceptance of its results."

General Raasloff's reply to this intimation is an illustration of the leisurely habits of the Danes. He said there was again a crisis in the Cabinet, *which he thought would be over within a week*, and *then* there would be nothing in the way of work. The General was also of opinion that, as Congress had adjourned, there was no occasion for haste.

Further negotiation revealed the fact only the more clearly, that Denmark would not yield the point of the vote in the Islands. Mr. Yeaman telegraphed to the Secretary of State on the second of October: "Denmark quite ready to conclude if vote mentioned in treaty. Considers favorable vote sure. Desires explicit acceptance of Santa Cruz."

To this Mr. Seward replied by telegraph: "No condition of vote in treaty. If Denmark wants to negotiate for Santa Cruz by separate treaty, send draft here for consideration."

A day or two after, Mr. Yeaman, learning that the French Minister was opposing the cession more warmly than usual, telegraphed thus to Mr. Seward: "France knows our offer and remonstrates. Denmark expects other remonstrances. Prompt action desirable. Vote in treaty indispensable."

Mr. Seward then yielded, and telegraphed to the American Minister in Copenhagen: "Concede question of vote."

But still the Danish Ministry hesitated. "They appear to me," wrote Mr. Yeaman, "to be really desirous of concluding, but to be timid and over nice, and unduly cautious about third

powers, and certain interests that might be affected by the cession." In truth, as Mr. Yeaman afterwards explained, the Cabinet was divided on the question of cession. When at last it came to the point of concluding, the Minister of Marine resigned his office, rather than be supposed to consent to it.

All things have an end. On the twenty-fourth of October, 1867, Mr. Yeaman was the happiest of men, for it was on that day that he had the pleasure of signing the treaty. It is evident from the whole tenor of his despatches that it cost the Danish Government a severe struggle to part with these Islands, and that in parting with them the Ministry honestly supposed that they were performing an act extremely and universally agreeable to the people of the United States. Nothing can be more certain than that they would have refused the cession absolutely, if they could have foreseen the humiliating delays and painful embarrassments to which they have since been subjected.

The negotiations, I may mention here, were stimulated in the course of the summer, by the arrival in Copenhagen of Senator Doolittle, who came charged with a secret mission from Mr. Seward, to give all the aid he could in bringing the affair to a successful issue. Mr. Doolittle's mere presence in Copenhagen was influential; for was he not a member of the body by whom the treaty would have to be ratified? But he contributed more than his presence. He actively and ably co-operated with Mr. Yeaman, and aided materially in overcoming the reluctance and hesitation of the Danish Government. Mr. Seward also requested the Russian Government to use its friendly offices to the same end, and this request was complied with. Such was the pressure brought by Mr. Seward to bear upon Denmark in aid of his scheme! And finally occurred the imposing visit of Admiral Farragut to Copenhagen, where he and the officers of his fleet were so warmly welcomed.

AN AMERICAN AGENT SENT TO THE ISLANDS.

On the twenty-fourth of October, 1867, then, the treaty was signed at Copenhagen by Count Frijs and George H. Yeaman. The transaction, however, was still far from being complete. The vote in the Islands remained to be taken; the treaty had still to be ratified by the Danish Parliament and by the American Senate; and, finally, it would be necessary for the House of Representatives to vote the money. Mr. Seward does not seem to have been apprehensive of difficulty in accomplishing any of these things, except the vote in the Islands. Accordingly, on the very day upon which he received the telegraphic announcement that the treaty had been signed, he initiated measures for disposing the inhabitants of the Islands to the transfer. He must have known that, when once the Danish Government had publicly and officially announced its willingness to transfer the Islands to the United States, and when the people of the Islands had expressed their willingness to be transferred, it would be extremely difficult, if not impossible, for Denmark to maintain that sovereignty over the Islands which she had so long wielded, and to which the benignity and justice of her rule entitled her. A decisive vote in favor of the United States would almost necessarily involve a severance from Denmark forever. Nevertheless, Mr. Seward, the most sanguine of men, pressed forward to a vote with even more than his usual alacrity.

October 26, 1867, he despatched to the Rev. Dr. Charles Hawley, of Auburn, New York, a curious and interesting letter: —

"This government," wrote the Secretary of State to his reverend friend, " has concluded a treaty with Denmark for a cesssion of the islands of St. Thomas and St John. . . . . It is understoood that the treaty contains a stipulation that before the cession shall be absolute the vote of the people of the Islands shall be taken upon the proposed change of sovereignty. It is also understood that the Danish Government has sent a commissioner for the purpose of superintending the taking of that vote. As it is desirable that this government should not be entirely without the attendance of a representative there, you are requested to proceed to St. Thomas. You will, however, consider your attendance there as of a character entirely confidential. But .... you are at liberty to present yourself to the Danish commissioner, and you will show him this instruction. ..... In all things you will practise the utmost frankness with him and absolute deference to his judgment and opinions. It is expected that you will meet Rear-Admiral Palmer, of the United States Navy, with the ship of war Susquehannah, at St. Thomas, who will have instructions similar to your own to co-operate with the Danish commissioner.

"It is presumed that you will be at no loss for arguments to show those who may have votes upon the subject the advantages they would derive from transferring their allegiance to the United States, should they think proper to remain in the Islands. The market of this country, even now, is an eligible one for their products. It must become much more so in the event of their annexation. As one of the purposes of this government in the acquisition is to secure a naval station, the inhabitants of the Islands will derive benefits from that, which it is needless to expatiate upon. If, too, they should become a part of the domain of the United States, they and their posterity will have the same right to protection by a powerful government in war, and to those advantages in the time of peace, which are enjoyed by other citizens."

In pursuance of this commission, Dr. Hawley reached St. Thomas on the twelfth of November, 1867. Chamberlain Carstensen, the Danish commissioner, arrived a few days after. Rumors of the purchase had preceded them, and the merchants were asking with anxiety, Will the United States continue St. Thomas a free port? for upon that they supposed its prosperity as a place of business depended. American men-of-war were in the harbor, and the inhabitants were all excitement and expectation. It was convenient for the commissioners to hold their first interview with the Island authorities at Christiansted in Santa Cruz, and Commodore Bissell of the Monongahela placed his vessel at their service for the purpose of transporting them thither.

THE EARTHQUAKE OF NOV. 18, 1867.

The interview was appointed to take place at the Government House at three o'clock in the afternoon of the eighteenth of November, — a day that will ever be remembered by the inhabitants of all the Islands in that portion of the Caribbean Sea. The commissioners had already assembled in the reception-room of the Government House. Suddenly the first shock of the terrible earthquake was felt. All present rushed in terror from the building. The whole population was in the streets, in that condition of panic of which no adequate idea can be formed by those who have never had such an experience. The waters at the first shock had receded from the shore, and were now seen returning in a huge wave, twenty feet high and stretching as far as the eye could reach, threatening to overwhelm the town. The people fled toward the hills for safety; but the mighty wave spent most of its force in breaking upon the reef at the harbor's mouth, and did less damage to the town than could have been supposed possible. The damage, however, was serious; some lives were lost; twenty or thirty buildings were destroyed; and the Monongahela was carried bodily from her anchorage, borne three quarters of a mile upon the summit of the wave, and left high and dry upon the land.

In these circumstances none of the gentlemen concerned were in the humor for the transaction of business, and the conference was deferred. It was an ominous commencement. Within the memory of man, St. Thomas had never before experienced an earthquake that could be called severe. On former occasions, when the West Indies were shaken by earthquakes, the shocks at St. Thomas had always been slight and harmless, so that the inhabitants built their houses, as may still be seen, without any reference to the likelihood of such a catastrophe. And although this earthquake was severe and long continued, yet the damage done was remarkably small, considering its violence; the new Government House at St. Thomas, composed wholly of stone, not exhibiting a single fissure. It was that mighty wave of the sea, caused by an upheaval elsewhere, which did most of the damage that day. Even from the hurricanes to which the West Indies are notoriously subject St. Thomas had been unusually exempt. Mr. Seward's treaty, however, being destined to encounter every possible mishap, both the earthquake and the hurricane of 1867 must needs be violent beyond all previous example.

THE VOTE POSTPONED.

For eleven days after the great convulsion, shocks were experienced every day, which, though they did no damage, kept the people in such alarm that little was accomplished by the commissioners. November 26, an informal conference was held in the Government House at St. Thomas between Governor Birch, Chamberlain Carstensen, Dr. Hawley, and other Americans on the one side, and the leading merchants of the Islands on the other. The conference lasted two hours. The merchants expressed themselves with perfect frankness, observing that, while they were more than willing to consent to the transfer, yet they were obliged to make their consent conditional upon St. Thomas remaining a free port, at least for some years. The business of the island was purely commercial; the town was only a kind of general depot of merchandise, to which all nations contributed, and from which all the adjacent islands and countries were supplied. To subject the commerce of the island to the tariff system of the United States would be to seriously injure that commerce.

Dr. Hawley could only reply to these representations, that he felt their reasonableness, but that the difficulty had not been anticipated in his instructions, and he had, therefore, no authority to give an assurance of the kind demanded.

The result of the conference was, that the Governor and commissioners concluded it unsafe to risk a vote at that time. Nor, indeed, had the terror caused by the earthquake sufficiently subsided. Some of the more ignorant of the inhabitants, who at St. Thomas, as everywhere else on earth, are superstitious, were disposed to attribute that catastrophe to the displeasure of Heaven at the contemplated change of sovereignty. For all reasons, delay was advisable. It was arranged that, before any further step was taken, Mr. Carstensen and Dr. Hawley should go to Washington in order to lay before Mr. Seward a statement of the merchants' wishes, and to endeavor to procure some kind of assurance that the port would remain free for a certain period, if not forever.

In the course of the conference, Chamberlain Carstensen read the proclamation of the King of Denmark to the people of the Islands, in which the King informed them of what had transpired. As this was an expression of the King's *wish* for a vote favorable to the United States, and as it was calculated to promote such a result, the proclamation was allowed to be published in the St. Thomas newspaper. Its publication was a proof of the confidence of the Danish Government in the reality of the sale, and in the honor of the United States. Every one who reads it must feel that the publication of such a document constituted, so far as Denmark was concerned, a *fait accompli*. It severed the tie. It broke that mystic spell which enables a man or a few men in one hemisphere to exercise control over whole communities in another. It was one of those acts which in their nature are irreversible. The following is a copy of the proclamation: —

ROYAL PROCLAMATION TO THE INHABITANTS OF THE ISLANDS OF ST. THOMAS AND ST. JOHN.

We, Christian the Ninth, by the grace of God King of Denmark, the Vandals, and the Goths, Duke of Schleswig, Holstein, Stormaru, Ditmarsh, Lauenburg, and Oldenburg, send to our beloved and faithful subjects in the Islands of St. Thomas and St. John our royal greeting.

We have resolved to cede our Islands of St. Thomas and John to the United States of America, and we have to that end, with the reservation of the constitutional consent of our Rigsdag, concluded a convention with the President of the United States. We have, by embodying in that convention explicit and precise provisions, done our utmost to secure you protection in your liberty, your religion, your property, and private rights, and you shall be free to remain where you now reside or to remove at any time, retaining the property which you possess in the said Islands, or disposing thereof and removing the proceeds wherever you please, without you being subjected on this account to any contribution, tax, or charge whatever.

Those who shall prefer to remain in the said Islands may either retain the title and the rights of their natural allegiance or acquire those of citizens of the United States, but they shall make their choice within two years from the date of the exchange of ratifications of the said convention, and those who shall remain in the Islands after the expiration of that term without having declared their intention to retain their natural allegiance shall be considered to have chosen to become citizens of the United States.

As we, however, will not exercise any constraint over our faithful subjects, we will give you the opportunity of freely and extensively expressing your wishes in regard to this cession, and we have to that effect given the necessary instructions to our commissioner extraordinary.

With sincere sorrow do we look forward to the severment of those ties which for many years have united you to us and the mother country, and, never forgetting the many demonstrations of loyalty and affection we have received from you, we trust that nothing has been neglected upon our side to secure the future welfare of our beloved and faithful subjects, and that a mighty impulse, both moral and material, will be given to the happy development of the Islands under the new sovereignty. Commending you to God !

Given at our palace of Amalienborg, the 25th of October, 1867, under our royal hand and seal.

CHRISTIAN, R.

Upon this proclamation the editor of the St. Thomas newspaper commented in a spirit friendly to the object sought. He endeavored to quiet the apprehensions of the merchants. "The Americans," he said, in substance, " are not fools; they will see at a glance that high duties would annihilate the business of the Islands; and they are not the kind of people to do anything that is manifestly impolitic." "If," continued the editor, in his simple way, "the people of the Islands should exact pledges of the United States, the United States might very properly reply: 'You distrust us in advance! You doubt us at the threshold of the transaction! We have done with it. You can keep your Islands.'"

The editor pointed to the fact that thousands of people every week sought liberty and happiness in the United States, and urged that such a country needed no certificate of good character. "The freest country in the world," he said, "has no need to trumpet its professions in advance. Let the transaction be done, as the charter-parties say, *in good faith*, and we shall win the gratitude of Denmark and become the pet of the United States."

THE DANISH COMMISSIONER IN WASHINGTON.

In December, 1867, Mr. Carstensen and Dr. Hawley were conveyed to Washington in an armed vessel of the United States.

Mr. Seward could not, of course, make the concession which the merchants of St. Thomas desired. The United States, he remarked, in reply to the memorial on the subject, are an aggregation of forty-seven distinct political communities, thirty-seven of which are States, and ten are preparing to become States. All of them had once belonged to foreign nations; but such had been the benignant operation of self-government in the United States that not one of these communities could now be induced to assume independence, nor to return to its former allegiance, nor accept another sovereign.

During Mr. Carstensen's short stay in Washington, he endeavored to ascertain whether, in case the vote in the Islands should be favorable and the treaty should be ratified in Denmark, there would be any difficulty in procuring its ratification and execution in Washington. A resolution had been recently introduced into the House of Representatives designed to guard against future purchases of territory for the United States. Mr. Carstensen inquired of a distinguished member of Congress what this meant. To which the Honorable member replied in substance, "*It means nothing at all*, and will not be thought of when this question comes up."

Mr. Seward did not talk quite as plainly as this, but the commissioner gathered from him that he had no doubt whatever of the acceptance of the treaty by Congress. Mr. Carstensen left Washington *entirely* reassured. Every one he met said to him in effect, "*You do your part, and we will do ours.*"

He reached St. Thomas on the first of January, 1868, and entered at once upon preparations for taking the vote. On the fourth of January, he met at the Government House the merchants and others at whose instance he had visited Washington. He said to them that he had conveyed to the Secretary of State their memorial, and he could say to them, with regard to it, that the inhabitants of St. Thomas by annexation to the United States will secure rights superior even to those which they have so long enjoyed as a colony under the protection of Denmark.

"The impression," he continued, "which I bring with me from the United States is that the United States are determined on having a military and commercial station in the West Indies; if not at St. Thomas, then at some other West Indian locality. I bring with me the conviction that these plans involve the future mercantile prosperity of St. Thomas, and that the inhabitants of St. Thomas by opposing annexation might prejudice the future commercial position of St. Thomas."

THE VOTE TAKEN.

During these few weeks, the project of annexation had been constantly growing in favor with the islanders, until at length they seemed unanimous and enthusiastic for the change. The voting in St. Thomas occurred January 9, 1868. It was a universal holiday, and all the people were out of doors. Early in the morning, a long procession of voters bearing the American flag, and, preceded by a band of music playing Hail Columbia, marched to the polls accompanied by a great crowd of people. Blue was the American color. At eight o'clock in the morning, in the presence of the governor, the commissioner, and other distinguished persons, both Danish and American, the first ticket was deposited in the urn. It was a blue ticket, and was cast by James B. Gomez, a well-known native of the island, and proprietor of an estate. At the close of the day, it was found that one thousand and thirty-nine votes had been cast for the cession, and only twenty-two against it. On the following day the vote was taken in St. John, where there were two hundred and five votes in favor of the cession, and not one against it. All appeared delighted with the result. Bands and processions went about the towns all day, and serenades were given in the evening.

"The success of the blue ticket," said the local paper, "relieves both contracting parties from an embarrassing position, since it would have been hard to tell how the treaty could have been finally ratified on either side in the absence of a successful *plebiscitum*, — the only modern method by which one people may now be incorporated with another, and at the same time exempt the contractors from the odium of having handed over their citizens or subjects as simply materials for purchase and sale."

The editor also thought that, in this instance, the voters of St. Thomas had contrived to sit upon two stools without coming to the ground, since they had "conformed to the wishes of his Majesty the King, and at the same time seasonably met the wishes of the United States Government."

THE TREATY RATIFIED IN DENMARK.

Count Frijs, meanwhile, was beginning to be a little uneasy. Since the earthquake, articles had appeared in American papers adverse to the cession; and what was more to be dreaded, a good deal of damaging ridicule had been aimed at Mr. Seward's propensity to buy land, as well as at this particular purchase. The House resolution of November 25, 1867, designed to secure to the House its part of the treaty-making power, caused anxiety in Denmark, and Mr. Yeaman wrote respecting it to Mr. Seward, that "any favorable explanation of the matter, or any well-founded belief that the House will vote the money, could be used by me to good advantage here, and telegraphic communication might be well."

Count Frijs, in fact, was so much alarmed, that he told Mr. Yeaman that, after hearing of a favorable vote in the Islands, Denmark *would be fully committed*, and that in his opinion the treaty ought to be ratified by the Senate before he even presented it to the Parliament of Denmark. He even went further than this, and intimated to Mr. Yeaman that he might deem it best to take no further step until the House of Representatives had actually voted the money! Mr. Yeaman, however, always opposed delay. The House, said the American Minister, might well decline to vote the money until the treaty was ratified on both sides, but that *he did not remember a case in which the House had refused money to carry a ratified treaty into effect*. Upon this, Count Frijs agreed that it would not be necessary to wait for the action of the House, but he was still of the opinion that the Rigsdag ought not to ratify until the Senate had done so.

Our Senate, however, as we all know, was disposed to nothing so little as to act upon the Danish treaty. The treaty had been sent in on the third of December, 1867, and the Senate had been duly notified of the favorable result of the vote in the Islands, but the treaty remained in Mr. Sumner's pigeon-hole untouched. Mr. Seward, however, always hopeful, continued to represent the delay in the most favorable light. He reminded the Danish Ministry, through Mr. Yeaman, that, as this was the long session of Congress, "*no inference unfavorable to the success of the treaty could be drawn from the delay.*" He also informed Mr. Yeaman that an envoy from the Dominican

Republic was in Washington offering a harbor for sale, and observed that "it is not unlikely the Senate will prefer to wait for the result of my conferences with the Dominican Minister, before proceeding to a final consideration of the Danish treaty." Mr. Seward concluded this despatch with the statement, that "certainly the treaty for St. Thomas and St. John loses nothing in popular favor by a free examination of its merits."

In a private letter to Mr. Yeaman of the same date, Mr. Seward continued in the same joyous and hopeful strain, reminding Mr. Yeaman that Jefferson was assailed for twelve years on account of his purchase of Louisiana, and that no one now thought it unwise in the government to buy California.

"The sharpness of criticism," added Mr. Seward, "upon the acquisition of Alaska is manifestly abated already. The extension of the United States into the tropical seas is an affair scarcely less important than either of those. It would have been wonderful if it had escaped a searching popular investigation."

Such was the reassuring tone of Mr. Seward's despatches at this critical time. With regard to the allusion of Count Frijs to the action of the House of Representatives, he went a little further, and intimated, through Mr. Yeaman, that what the House of Representatives did or did not do in such a matter was none of Count Frijs's business. He couched this intimation in the following terms, not too polite : —

"It would not be becoming for me to entertain correspondence with a foreign state concerning incidental debates and resolutions in regard to the treaty for the two Danish Islands, while it is undergoing constitutional consideration in the Senate and in Congress. I may add that I think that it belongs to the Executive of Denmark, so that it always proceeds in good faith towards the United States, to determine when and how it will submit the treaty for consideration and ratification of the Rigsdag; and when he shall so have submitted it, that the current debates it shall call forth in the Danish Legislature will not probably be made the subject of attention by the President of the United States."

This despatch, I am informed, was influential with the Danish Ministry. There was the tone of the *master* in it. How could the Danish Ministry suppose that a Secretary of State who held such language as this could have a reasonable treaty rejected? They agreed, at length, that, since Denmark was already fully and publicly committed to the transfer of the Islands, it would be useless and ungracious to delay the completion of their part of the contract. Count Frijs, accordingly, a few days after receiving intelligence of the favorable result of the voting, submitted the treaty to the Rigsdag, by whom it was promptly ratified. The treaty was signed on the same day, June 31, 1868, by the King. On the day following, Mr. Yeaman telegraphed to the Secretary of State: "Treaty sent to Washington ratified by Rigsdag and signed by King." To which he added in cipher: "Several European Powers hope it will fail in Congress."

On the second of February, 1868, the Senate of the United States was officially informed of the ratification of the treaty by the King and Parliament of Denmark. The Senate adjourned, however, without acting upon it, and nothing has since been done in the matter. The time named in the treaty for the exchange of ratifications was four months from the date of its conclusion, and that term expired February 24, 1868.

When the Senate had adjourned without acting upon the Danish treaty, Mr. Seward asked the Danish Government for another year. In according this solicited privilege, Count Frijs requested M. Bille, the Danish Chargé at Washington, to inform Mr. Seward of the loss and embarrassment which the delay in ratifying the treaty had caused and were causing. The prolongation, he said, of the state of suspense seriously affected the interests of the people of the Islands, and "places his Majesty's Government in a painful and unforeseen position." In reply Mr. Seward said: "I am directed by the President to acknowledge the *force and propriety* of the considerations expressed in that communication, and to assure you that such further proceedings as are necessary to give full effect to the treaty will be taken *with good faith and diligence* on the part of the United States."

Has this promise been kept? Was any attempt made to keep it? I believe not. And yet, reader, it was made on behalf of THE UNITED STATES, by a man whom foreign governments were obliged to accept as our spokesman and authoritative agent!

The additional year conceded by Denmark to Mr. Seward's solicitation expires on the fifteenth of October, 1869.

SUMMARY OF THE FOREGOING.

The narrative just concluded shows, among other things, the following: —

1. It was the Government of the United States that initiated the negotiations for the cession of the Islands.
2. Denmark was unwilling to sell them, and there were weighty reasons of policy against selling them to the United States.
3. In selling them to the United States, Denmark deliberately preferred a closer alliance with the United States to a closer alliance with England and France.
4. Denmark accepted a lower price than she at first deemed just, and that price was the one offered by the United States.
5. Denmark had no reason to suppose that this acquisition was not as heartily desired by the people of the United States as it was manifestly desirable.
6. Denmark, trusting to the good faith of the Government of the United States, has taken steps toward the transfer of the Islands which cannot, in the nature of things, be retraced.

THE INJURY TO DENMARK IN CASE THE TREATY IS NOT RATIFIED AND EXECUTED.

I call the attention of the reader to this point here, because it is one upon which a difference of opinion is hardly possible. That Denmark will suffer serious loss and damage if we do not accept and execute the treaty is manifest, but it is not manifest *how* serious that loss and damage may be. She will be humiliated in the eyes of all the vulgar part of mankind, whose habit it is to sneer at the victims of unworthy conduct, not at the party guilty of the same. Denmark, as Mr. Yeaman remarked, after the heavy losses of the last few years, has the feeling of being abandoned by her natural allies, and abandoned because she is weak. Now comes this last stroke. She sees Alaska paid for, because Russia is a powerful friend whom we will not run the risk of estranging, while her own treaty, negotiated in the same manner by the same person, and for objects more important, lies unnoticed. Such treatment, when it cannot be effectively resented, tends to lower a people's self-respect, and diminish their moral and physical force. There is perhaps no offence more damaging than an unjust wound to a reasonable self-love.

We are also to consider that it was the liberal and progressive party of Denmark which carried this measure, and that that party is both weakened and dishonored if we repudiate the treaty. General Raasloff might well say, as he did some time since : —

" I am morally responsible for having persuaded the Danish Government to cause the vote to be taken, — an act which nothing but the most implicit confidence in the good faith of the United States, and in the binding character of the treaty, could justify, and which now threatens the most disastrous consequences to my too confiding country." And again : " Having been more than anybody else instrumental in bringing such a calamity and humiliation down upon my country, I shall have proved myself utterly unfit to be a constitutional adviser of the Crown. If it was folly to believe in the good faith of the United States, I and my colleagues ought to suffer for that folly."

Every one will agree that, in order to stand justified before mankind for putting to an open shame the ablest and most progressive statesmen of Denmark, we must be able to adduce reasons which the judgment of an impartial world will approve, and international usages justify.

Especially must we bear in mind that Denmark has already experienced a considerable portion of the loss involved in the cession of the Islands. She has *shown* her willingness to disoblige England, France, and Spain, and she has *shown* a preference for the friendship of the United States. This damage has been done. Her feelings have gone into irrevocable print. She has publicly given in her adherence to the great powers of the Future, and disregarded the wishes of the great powers of the Past. She has given the latter a pretext for disregarding *her* interests in future complications. Nor is it certain that she has not lost her Islands, whether we pay for them or not. Did not General Butler, the other day, in Congress, intimate a willingness to consider the vote of the islanders in the light of an accomplished cession ?

"We have," remarked General Butler, " by our action put ourselves in a very anomalous position in regard to some of these Islands. Our Executive called upon Denmark, and asked to have the people of St. Thomas vote whether they would belong to Denmark or to this country. That people voted that they preferred to belong to this country, and thereupon they seem to have shut themselves off from Denmark, while we are not yet ready or willing to ratify the treaty by which we agreed to pay money for that island."

These were ominous words. The reader of the foregoing pages perceives that General Butler was not aware, when he uttered them, of one of the most material facts concerning the treaty and the Island vote. But there is no man in Congress who would go further than General Butler in fulfilling the conditions of a just compact between the United States and a foreign power. I look, therefore, with confidence to seeing him support and vote for the execution of this treaty when it comes to be acted upon by the House, of which he is so efficient a member. I quote his words merely to show that the hold which Denmark had upon those Islands is weakened by the treaty of cession. Many circumstances, highly probable, can be imagined in which St. Thomas would be immediately wrested from any but a first-rate naval power. Great changes are imminent in the West Indies. Those fertile islands are about to begin to play their proper part in the affairs of this continent. Without going into detail on this interesting branch of the subject, I would submit it as a question to the intelligence of every candid reader acquainted with human affairs: Is it not clear that the act to which General Butler refers in his remarks quoted above, namely, the vote in the Islands of January, 1868, can never be wholly undone?

I would also remind the reader that seven millions and a half in gold is to Denmark about what three hundred millions of dollars in currency would be to the United States. In other words, it is nearly a year's revenue. The population of Denmark is now sixteen hundred thousand, and its annual revenue is a little more than eight millions of dollars.

AND WHAT IS DENMARK?

Denmark is a power which, in everything but magnitude, wealth, and numbers, compares advantageously with the four most advanced nations of the earth. Without indulging in vague eulogium, I will mention two or three circumstances which give to this little Kingdom a special claim to the respectful consideration of the United States.

Denmark is one of the few free countries of the world. Its government is a strictly limited constitutional monarchy, with a Legislature composed of two Houses. I believe there is no region of the earth in which the natural rights of man are held more sacred than in Denmark, nor one in which a larger proportion of the people enjoy substantial welfare. An honest attempt is made in that country to educate the whole people. The means of education are provided for all, and no child can be defrauded of education by parent, guardian, or master, or by his own negligence, except in violation of the law. Copenhagen, considering the slender revenues of the Kingdom, is wonderfully rich in galleries of art, museums, libraries, collections of coins and other instructive objects. Its University is highly respectable. Copenhagen is the city of Oersted, Thorwaldsen, Andersen, — three names of universal celebrity, and each the representative and ornament of a numerous body.

The course of Denmark with regard to the colored population of her Islands would alone entitle her to the respect of the human family. In 1792, she took the lead of all the nations in abolishing the slave-trade! In 1848 she abolished slavery throughout her dominions, but long before doing so she instituted a series of measures designed to prepare the slaves for the perilous gift of freedom. She dotted her Islands all over with school-houses, and made the attendance of the colored children for a certain portion of the year, and for a term of years, obligatory. The Danish laws regulating the treatment of the slaves were so mild and just that, when at length the day of emancipation came, neither whites nor blacks were conscious of any great change. It is the universal testimony of persons familiar with the West Indies, that no where are the colored people so happy, so well cared for, so well protected by the law, as in the Danish Islands. I have conversed with several highly intelligent gentlemen who have resided there, and they all bear witness to this fact. Mr. Seward said, when he returned from his visit to them a few years ago: "At Santa Cruz I saw for the first time the colored people as I wish to see them."

Nearly four years before his visit, the attention of the Government of the United States had been forcibly called to the happy and truly fortunate condition of the colored people in the Danish Islands, and it had entered into a convention, negotiated by the Danish Minister and the Secretary of Interior, for the settlement in Santa Cruz of blacks taken from captured slavers by American men-of-war. Our government became satisfied that this was far more humane than sending them to their native continent, where they were almost certain to be reduced again to slavery, and were very likely to be sold again to the traders for transportation to the Spanish possessions. I have read the laws relating to the laboring population of the Danish islands, and they appear well adapted to secure the rights and happiness of a people recently emancipated, and not yet a generation removed from total ignorance. The operation of those wise and just laws prevented the Danish Islands from lapsing into the condition of Jamaica, where the emancipation of the slaves was very far from being an unmixed good. Jamaica, as we all remember, was a standing argument against freedom, — an argument of which the Danish Islands were a complete refutation, though at the time we were not aware of it.

Perhaps to this brief indication of the solid merits of Denmark it may not be improper to add a few words respecting its reigning family. The present king, Christian IX., is an exemplary and truly respectable character, a man of amiable disposition and strong domestic attachments. He has performed the very difficult task — more difficult for a king than for any other man — of rearing a large family so well that his children reflect honor upon their race and country wherever they go. One of his daughters, the Princess Alexandra, so beloved by the people among whom she dwells, will one day be Queen of England, and promises to give that support to the throne by her virtues and good sense which we have reason to fear it will need. Another of the daughters of this royal house is the wife of that Russian prince who is heir-apparent to the imperial throne. A son of King Christian is interesting to us as King of Greece.

In every point of view, Denmark is the last of the powers to whose rights and feelings the United States should be indifferent.

There is a good deal of cant written about the friendship of one government for another. I do not know that there is any such thing as friendship between governments. A government is merely *intrusted* with the power and resources of a country, and it is bound to use that power and those resources with a single eye to the true and permanent welfare of the country governed. A government, perhaps, can never properly be generous; certainly, it ought always to be just. On several remarkable occasions, however, the Government of Denmark has shown that it felt itself morally akin to that of the United States. I remember that, as far back as 1783, just after the close of the Revolution, the Prime Minister of Denmark wrote to the Danish Envoy at Paris a letter abounding in sympathy with what he styled "the glorious issue" of our Revolutionary War.

"I cannot omit," wrote this Minister to the Envoy, "warmly recommending to you to endeavor, during your stay at Paris, to gain as much as possible the esteem and confidence of Dr. Franklin. You will recollect what I said in my conversations with you of the high respect all the King's Ministry have for that Minister. You have witnessed the satisfaction with which we have learned the glorious issue of this war for the United States, and how fully we are persuaded that it will be for the general interest of the two states to form, as soon as possible, reciprocal conventions of commerce and friendship."

Such conventions were speedily concluded. The ancient Kingdom and the young Republic became cordial allies, since both were subject to the same danger and had the same interests. Both were weak nations contending for their rights as neutrals amid the conflicts of the most powerful empires in the world. Count Bernstoff, the Prime Minister of Denmark, who wrote the letter quoted above, was the eminent European champion of the rights of neutrals, to whom they all looked for counsel and moral support. And yet, in the course of the long and imbittered wars between the allies and Napoleon, when Denmark and the United States had so difficult parts to play, many seizures were made of American vessels (sailing under British convoy or with British licenses) by Danish ships of war, and condemned, as the owners deemed, unjustly. These seizures led to a long negotiation between Denmark and the United States for the redress of that grievance. The affair was finally arranged while the distinguished Mr. Wheaton represented the United States at Copenhagen. It was a really difficult case, as may be seen by reference to Mr. Wheaton's work upon International Law, and some eminent lawyers are to this day of opinion that Denmark was not legally responsible for the injury done. The Danish Government, however, waived the technicalities of the case, and settled the matter by paying, for distribution among the owners of the captured vessels, six hundred and fifty thousand dollars, besides relinquishing important claims of their own against us.

Many particulars could here be given of the conduct of Denmark during the late war, — I mean the war which was fought *out* on land between the United States and the Southern Confederacy, and fought on the sea between the United States and Great Britain, — which would show that the heart of Denmark in that great contest was *not* with the power which bombarded her capital and carried off her fleet sixty years ago. Mr. Seward himself testified to the friendship of the Danish Government in a despatch of June 9, 1863, when he said that its "just and *liberal* consideration of our rights is acknowledged with peculiar satisfaction." No matter for this. I merely wish to insist that, in all the diplomatic intercourse which has occurred between the two countries, from 1783 to the present time, the conduct of the Danish Government has always been strictly honorable, courteous, and more than ordinarily friendly.

Denmark now has one more claim to our respectful consideration, which will appeal powerfully to every mind not incapable of magnanimity. She is clad in the sacred majesty of weakness and undeserved misfortune. We can rob these jewels from her if we will. But if, after paying for Alaska, we refuse to stand to our bargain for St. Thomas and St. John, it will be hard to convince mankind that we paid Russia for any other reason than because Russia is strong, and that we decline to pay Denmark for any other reason than because Denmark is weak.

BUT IS THE BARGAIN OURS?

That is the main question! Is it *our* bargain, and not merely Mr. Seward's?

A treaty of this kind, which stipulates the payment of money by the United States, requires a double ratification: the Senate must ratify the treaty, and the House must vote the money. There is an impression in some circles that Congress has the same right to give or withhold this twofold ratification that it has to pass or reject any ordinary measure of legislation. Whether this ought or ought not to be the case is not the question to be considered here. I have only to say that such a right has never been claimed by a majority in Congress, nor exercised by Congress nor by any other legislative body.

According to all American precedent, the Senate has the same kind of right to refuse the ratification of a treaty which it has to reject a nomination sent in by the President; and the House has the same kind of right to refuse the money for the execution of a treaty which it has to reject a bill appropriating money for the necessary expenses of the government.

The Senate *may* refuse to confirm an appointment for reasons of pique or prejudice. It has the *power* to do this, as a strong man sometimes has the power to trample upon the rights of the weak. But before the Senate can reject a nomination rightfully, sound and solid reasons must be adduced. Some senator or senators must rise and say in substance: " The man nominated resides in my district, and I personally know him to be untrustworthy and incapable." Or he must say : " The previous incumbent of the office I personally know to have been honest and competent, and I know that he was removed for his merits, and not for his faults." When senators of known integrity give information of this kind, the Senate not only has a moral right to reject the nomination, but is morally bound to reject it.

The House, also, would, in certain possible contingencies, be justified in rejecting an appropriation bill which would absolutely bring the government to a stand-still. But in no ordinary circumstances would it be justified in doing this. Such a course would savor of revolution ; it would be of the nature of a last resort ; it would in no proper sense of the word be legislation.

It was only the other day that I myself heard a distinguished member of Congress, in speaking of an item in the Indian Appropriation Bill, use language illustrative of this point. He was remarking upon the immense difficulties which General

Grant would experience in carrying out his simple and patriotic programme of honestly administering the government.

"Why," said he, "look at this clause in our Indian Bill. I know, and the committee knows, and Congress believes, that the Indians will never get three tenths of this money, or the goods directed to be bought with it; and yet we must all vote for it."

"Must," said I, "why must?"

"Because we are bound to do it by a treaty."

A very little reflection, indeed, will show any one that the power which Congress rightfully has over treaties is essentially different from that which it has over the bills usually submitted to its consideration. According to the system established in all constitutional countries, a treaty may be rejected only for certain causes which are enumerated by the writers upon international law; the chief cause being a serious departure from the instructions of the minister who signed it.

Vattel, for example, says: "To refuse with honor to ratify that which has been concluded in virtue of a full power, the sovereign must have strong and solid reasons for it, and particularly he must show that his minister transcended his instructions."

Martens says: "Everything that has been stipulated by an agent, in conformity to his full powers, ought to become obligatory for the state from the moment of his signing, without ever waiting for the ratification. However, not to expose the state to errors of a single person, it is now become a general maxim, that public conventions do not become obligatory until ratified. The motive of this custom clearly proves that the ratification can never be refused with justice, except when he who is charged with the negotiation, keeping within the extent of his public full powers, has gone beyond his (secret) instructions, and consequently rendered himself liable to punishment; or when the other party refuse to ratify."

Wheaton says: "No institutional writer has laid down so lax a principle as that the ratification of a treaty, concluded in conformity with a full power, may be refused at the mere caprice of one of the contracting parties, and without assigning strong and solid reasons for such refusal."

I will not multiply citations, because, as far as I know, no respectable authority has ever maintained that a legislature has a moral right to withhold its sanction from a treaty properly concluded, except for stronger reasons than those of convenience. It is an axiom of business, both public and private, that a duly authorized agent, acting in conformity with his instructions, must never be disavowed.

A distinguished Senator put a searching question some time since to General Raasloff: —

"In your opinion," asked the Senator, "would the United States have a right to complain if your Rigsdag had refused *their* consent to the ratification of the St. Thomas treaty?"

An excellent question. The reply of the General was interesting and deserves consideration.

"If," said he, "the Rigsdag had refused their consent to the ratification of the treaty with the United States, the Danish Government would have dissolved that body, and appealed to the people by means of a general election; and if the new Rigsdag, elected on that question, should likewise have refused their consent, the Cabinet ministers would have resigned their offices. But even though we should in that manner have given you all the satisfaction our government had it in their power to give, you would, in my opinion, still have a right to complain of us for having trifled with you in having neglected to secure beforehand the ratification of a solemn treaty entered into with you; and that your right to complain would have been greater if the treaty had been made at our instigation, and greater still, if, implicitly confiding in the good faith of Denmark, the United States had *irrevocably committed themselves* by the adoption and execution of important measures which could not be deferred without rendering impossible the punctual exchange of ratifications within the term stipulated by the treaty itself."

This reply appears to meet the objection suggested by the honorable Senator's inquiry.

Perhaps it will elucidate this subject a little if I employ here a homely illustration. Let us suppose the United States to be a great mercantile firm established in the city of New York, of which firm William H. Seward is the managing partner, known to be such in the business circles of every commercial city on earth. He is identified with the house, whose name he is authorized to sign, and for whom he has made many important contracts and bargains, which have been fulfilled to the letter without question. George H. Yeaman, we will suppose, is the resident agent of this great firm at Calcutta. Mr. Seward writes to Mr. Yeaman a letter, which he is authorized to exhibit to parties interested, empowering and ordering him to buy for the firm a thousand chests of indigo at the lowest market rate, and ship the same to New York. Mr. Yeaman buys the indigo, places it on board ship, and notifies Mr. Seward. Can the firm rightfully repudiate the contract? They can; but only for causes recognized as sufficient by the commercial world. If it can be shown that Mr. Yeaman bought the indigo at a price much above the market rate, induced thereto by corrupt means, or had in any other way criminally violated a material part of his instructions, the house could properly, and with the approval of the mercantile community, disavow the purchase. But the bargain could not be disavowed because indigo had fallen in price, or because money was scarce, or for any other reason of mere convenience.

It is not in place to say here that Mr. Seward *ought not* to have been intrusted with such powers. It may be that a manager ought, in each transaction, to be required to call together the heads of the firm, to lay the matter before them, and secure a particular authorization before writing to a foreign agent. Arrange it so for the future if you will, and give due notice to your correspondents abroad. But these Islands were purchased on the system established, universal, and never before seriously called in question. Grant, if you please, that the firm did not want so much indigo, having a whole warehouse filled with it already. They must hold Mr. Seward responsible for that mistake. They must not exact the penalty from those worthy merchants, Messrs. Frijs, Raasloff, & Co., who sold their indigo at Mr. Seward's pressing request, at rates more favorable than they deemed quite just to themselves, and in disregard of the wishes of some old friends of their house, and now, having put the indigo on board ship, and made known the price at which they sold it, cannot take it back without incurring loss and shame.

As governments are now constructed, there must be an Executive which alone can treat with the governments of other nations. If Congress *has* unlimited power over treaties, — power to accept or reject them at pleasure, — then it is with *Congress* that foreign ministers will really negotiate. They may for a while maintain the forms of diplomatic intercourse with the Secretary of State, but they will put forth their strength and exercise their art in the lobbies and committee-rooms of the Capitol. The Government of the United States alone will have no means of holding effective intercourse with other governments, because every act of an American diplomatist will be vitiated by the known possibility of its being disavowed by the national Legislature for causes which a foreign minister can neither anticipate nor understand, and which the Legislature itself may not choose to explain. The caprice of a majority, the pique of a faction, the unpopularity of a president, indolence, fatigue, whim, artifice, may consign the most just and politic treaty to the tomb of the Speaker's table. A representative of the Government of the United States could not, in such circumstances, either associate with the ministers of foreign governments as an equal, or transact business with them on advantageous terms. An agent who fears to be disavowed, or who is known to be liable to that dishonor, cannot be expected to render efficient service. It is much if he is allowed to converse, hat in hand, with the heads of great houses of business. He is a mere correspondent, not an agent. His affair is to transmit information, not to sign contracts binding on his principals.

We must think twice before making such a change as this. At present, the government consists of *three* branches: Are we quite sure that we could manage better with two?

AMERICAN PRECEDENTS.

There is no case on record which is precisely similar to that of the treaty now under consideration. The question, however, of the duty of Congress with regard to the ratification and execution of treaties has received frequent illustration in the history of our diplomacy.

The Jay treaty of 1794 was, beyond all comparison, the most odious one to the American people that has ever been concluded between the United States and a foreign power. Mr. Jay was sent to England to procure, if possible, the admission of American wheat, fish, and meat into the ports of Great Britain on fair terms of reciprocity, to put an end to the impressment of American sailors and the lawless seizure of American cargoes, and to place the entire commercial intercourse of the two nations upon a just and equal footing. His treaty secured none of these objects. It was not in accordance with his instructions. It obliged *us* to pay damages to England, instead of compelling the English to pay damages to us. It left American sailors the unprotected prey of English captains. It gave us scarcely anything that we wanted, unless it was something we had already; and it denied us almost everything we wanted, unless it was something which we could not be prevented from taking. Never was there a treaty so revolting to a free people as this. The only thing that could be said in favor of it was: It was the best that could then be had! Mr. Jefferson thought so ill of it that he said we had better have no treaty at all than one which dishonored the infant nation. He thought we had better even "abolish the treaty-making power, except to conclude a peace," than accept it. It was fortunate, he added, that the first decision respecting the power of Congress over a treaty was "to be in a case so palpably atrocious as to have been predetermined by all America; for *on the precedent now to be set will depend the future construction of our Constitution.*"

The precedent *was* set. President Washington, after his

usual careful and deliberate consideration, ratified the treaty. Exactly two thirds of the Senate ratified it and the appropriations necessary for the execution of the treaty were passed in the House of Representatives by fifty-one to forty-eight. The opinion of Mr. Jefferson and of his friends in Congress was this: " When a treaty is made involving matters confided by the Constitution to the three branches of the Legislature conjointly, the representatives are as free as the President and Senate were to consider whether the national interest requires or forbids their giving the forms and force of law to the articles over which they have a power."

This was the popular doctrine of the day; but Congress did not act upon it, and all the precedents since are adverse to it. The time may come when we shall accept Mr. Jefferson's view of this matter; but as we cannot make an *ex post facto* law, so I conclude we cannot justly apply an *ex post facto* interpretation of law to the injury of an ally. The Jay treaty, I admit, gave the death-blow to the Federal party; but no Democratic majority has since failed to ratify a treaty properly made in accordance with instructions and with fundamental principles.

President Monroe and the whole country, Federalists and Democrats, were extremely indignant when the King of Spain refused to ratify the Florida cession treaty of 1819. The King, it seems, during the negotiations, had disposed of all the best land in Florida in "grants" to favored individuals, and these grants he desired should be recognized in the treaty of cession. The American Minister, of course, objected to purchase an estate thus encumbered, and the King, in consequence, refused to ratify. The language which Mr. Monroe held on this subject in his next message is curiously applicable to the Danish treaty.

"The treaty itself," said Mr. Monroe, "was formed on great consideration, and a thorough knowledge of all the circumstances; the subject-matter of every article having been for years under discussion, and repeated references having been made by the Minister of Spain to his government on the points respecting which the greatest difference of opinion prevailed. It was formed by a Minister duly authorized for the purpose, who had represented his government in the United States, and been employed in this long protracted negotiation several years; and who, it is not denied, kept strictly within the letter of his instructions. *The faith of Spain was therefore pledged, under circumstances of peculiar force and solemnity, for its ratification.*"

It was agreed throughout Christendom, that the King of Spain, in refusing to ratify, was guilty of an outrage against the United States; and I know, from unpublished letters, that, if General Jackson had been President, instead of James Monroe, he would have seized Florida! The Emperor of Russia, then, as always, the friend of the United States, fearing a breach of the peace, wrote to his Minister in Washington, that, "though he would not take it upon himself to justify Spain," yet he charged his Minister " to *plead* with the government at Washington the cause of peace and concord." " Some uneasiness was felt," says Mr. Lyman, the author of a work on the diplomacy of the United States, " lest the United States should resent the delay of Spain, and take possession of the Floridas by force." The same respectable author adds the following remarks : —

" This transaction is, we believe, without a precedent in the diplomacy of the United States. The government has refused to ratify treaties. Other nations have exercised the same privilege, but never without a reason; perhaps not in all cases satisfactory to the opposite party, but at least bearing upon its face some sort of defence and justification."

General Jackson's controversy with the government of Louis Philippe had much in it which resembled our present affair with Denmark, only in that case it was *we* who were to receive the money, and another power that had to pay it. In 1831, Mr. Rives, the American Minister at Paris, concluded a treaty with France, by which the French Government agreed to pay the United States five millions of dollars, in compensation for the unlawful seizure of American ships before the peace of 1815. We, on our part, agreed to settle some outstanding claims of French citizens against the United States, one of which (the claim of the heirs of Beaumarchais) dated back to the second year of the Revolutionary War. We also agreed to lower the duties on French wines to six cents per gallon for clarets, ten cents for white wines, and twenty-two cents for all bottled wines.

This treaty was duly ratified by President Jackson and the Senate of the United States. More than that,— Congress passed a law reducing the duties on French wines to the rates named in the treaty, appointed commissioners to distribute the money justly among the several claimants, and did all other acts and things requisite for the fulfilment of our part of the contract. Louis Philippe also ratified the treaty, and then nothing remained but for the French Chambers to vote the money. But they did not vote the money. At first, as this appeared to be merely the result of oversight or carelessness, President Jackson respectfully remonstrated. Then the Chambers took offence, and deliberately voted down the bill appropriating the money for the first instalment. No one who has any knowledge of the character of General Jackson needs to be informed what his feelings were when the news of this refusal of the money reached Washington. His message of 1834, though couched in the formal language usual in such documents, is a warlike paper indeed.

. "The idea," said the fiery chieftain, "of acquiescing in the refusal to execute the treaty will not, I am confident, be for a moment entertained by any branch of this government; and further negotiation is equally out of the question."

And further on: "It is my conviction that the United States ought to insist on a prompt execution of the treaty, and, in case it be refused or longer delayed, take redress into their own hands. . . . . I recommend that a law be passed authorizing reprisals upon French property in case provision shall not be made for the payment of the debt at the approaching session of the French Chambers."

There can be no doubt whatever that General Jackson would have precipitated the country into a war with France, had not the English Government, in the nick of time, offered its mediation. This was accepted, and the affair was speedily arranged, — the French Government paying the money, principal and interest.

It seems to me that this is, in several essential points, a case parallel with that of the Danish treaty. The United States, like Denmark, had completely fulfilled *their* part of the compact, and were so committed that the delay on the part of France was both an injury and an insult to them. We all know that, if Denmark had treated us as we are treating Denmark, we should regard her conduct, not, perhaps, with the boiling fury of General Jackson, but at least with all the indignation becoming a civilized people. If to-day a war should become imminent with a great naval power, does any one doubt that we should instantly consider the Islands ours, and send, in the same week, a fleet to St. Thomas and a small cartload of gold to the Danish legation? And if that naval power should offer Denmark twenty millions for her Islands, should we stand by quietly and witness the transfer?

THE VALUE OF THE ISLANDS. — DO WE WANT THEM?

The West Indies slant from the western extremity of Cuba toward the southwest, and extend in a waving line about twenty-five hundred miles. The whole number of islands is about one thousand, only forty-five of which, however, are of any considerable magnitude or value. They contain nearly one hundred thousand square miles, or, in other words, they comprise about twice as much land as Pennsylvania. A large portion of this territory is of the greatest fertility, and produces naturally the fruits, woods, and other commodities, such as coffee, spices, and sugar, for which mankind are willing to pay the highest price. The islands abound in tolerable harbors, and boast a very few excellent ones. The climate of many of the islands is perfectly salubrious and singularly enjoyable, and they exhibit natural scenes in the highest degree striking and picturesque.

All of these islands, except one, acknowledge the sovereignty of some foreign power; and every great naval power of the world exercises dominion over some of them, excepting alone the United States, to which they belong more naturally than to any other. Spain holds the largest of them under her sway. Over a large number — over most of the best of them — the flag of Great Britain floats. France possesses several; Holland, a few; Sweden has one; Venezuela, a small South American State, possesses one. But there is not an island in the West Indies where an American can live, except by sufferance, nor a harbor to which, in time of war, an American captain can take in a prize, or coal his ship, or haul up for repairs. And yet, to a great extent, those islands depend upon us for food, and we supply them with a large part of their machinery, fabrics, furniture, and articles of ornament and luxury. Every American ship which trades with South America, on either side of it, or with California, Oregon, and Alaska; every whaling-ship that makes its way to and from the fishing-grounds of the Pacific, passes by or among these islands, and is liable to require from them shelter and supplies.

The loss which accrued to the United States from the fact that, while we possessed no harbor in the West Indies, our naval enemy possessed several, and one within half a day's sail of the Florida coast, is beyond computation.

We all hope, of course, that there will never be another war between the United States and a great naval power, nor any other power. We are apt to think that defeated Toryism will give it up without another fight; but as Toryism is an indestructible ingredient of human nature, this hope is probably fallacious. It seems as if there were a necessity in the nature of things for every nation to have a great fight once in each generation. It seems as though war is a necessity which can only be outgrown, if at all, after many ages of progressive civilization. But whether we fight soon or late or never, the exigencies of peace make it highly desirable for the United States to possess a haven in the West Indies. The Darien Canal, which is likely to be our next great project, will throw into the family of nations all the States of the Pacific shore, will bring Valparaiso within twelve days' sail of New York, and will open to our commerce ten thousand miles of inhabited coast. Perhaps no work ever undertaken by man has produced so many, so important, and so permanent changes in the world's business, as the completion of a canal through the Isthmus of Darien promises to effect. There are able and patriotic men connected with this scheme, who live but to accomplish it, and we may rest assured that, from this time forward, it is destined to go on steadily towards realization. We must have a port in the West Indies, if only to aid in executing this undertaking; and when it is done, the necessity will be too obvious for remark.

The Danish Islands are situated about midway in the long waving line of the West Indies. They are three in number, and are named St. Thomas, St. John, and Santa Cruz. The largest and the most productive is the one last named, with which we have nothing at present to do. Santa Cruz, I may however mention in passing, is twenty miles long and five wide, measures one hundred and ten square miles, contains twenty-five thousand inhabitants, and produces about eleven thousand hogsheads of sugar per annum. St. Thomas is little more than a huge mass of rocks, twelve miles long and three broad, and contains thirteen thousand inhabitants, whose chief support is commerce. St. John is an island of about the same size, character, and population. Both St. Thomas and St. John have excellent defensible harbors, and are important to us solely on that account.

Respecting the particular value of those harbors, and their adaptedness to the wants of the United States, it were presumption in a landsman, and one of no commercial experience, to hazard an opinion. In such a matter we *must* depend upon the judgment of professional persons, such as the admirals and captains of our navy, the masters of clipper ships, and the heads of mercantile houses engaged in the West India trade. So far as I can ascertain, the opinion of such persons is, that, next to Havana, the harbor of St.

Thomas is the best in the West Indies, and in some respects better for *our* purposes even than Havana. Admiral Farragut has the highest opinion of the value of this harbor to the United States, and entirely approves the project of its acquisition. Vice-Admiral David D. Porter has placed his opinion upon record: —

"St. Thomas," he writes, "lies right in the track of all vessels from Europe, Brazil, East Indies, and the Pacific Ocean, bound to the West India Islands or to the United States. It is the point where all vessels touch for supplies, when needed, coming from any of the above stations. It is a central point from which any or all of the West India Islands can be assailed, while it is impervious to attack from landing parties, and can be fortified to any extent. The bay, at the head of which lies the town of St. Thomas, is almost circular, the entrance being by a neck, guarded by two heavy forts, which, although not capable at present of resisting the heavy ordnance now in use, can be so strengthened and protected that no foreign power could ever hope to take it.

"St. Thomas is a small Gibraltar of itself, and could only be attacked by a naval force. There would be no possibility of landing troops there, as the island is surrounded by reefs and breakers, and every point near which a vessel or boat could approach is a natural fortification, and only requires guns, with little labor expended on fortified works.

"There is no harbor in the West Indies better fitted than St. Thomas for a naval station. Its harbor and that of St. John, and the harbors formed by Water Island, would contain all the vessels of the largest navy in the world, where they would be protected at all times from bad weather, and be secure against an enemy.

"The people have always been our friends. During the Rebellion, when all the ports of the French and British West India Islands were closed against us, St. Thomas furnished our vessels with supplies of all kinds, gave us information, and turned the cold shoulder to the Rebel cruiser. They offered the latter no facilities for preying upon our commerce.

"In fine, I think St. Thomas is the keystone to the arch of the West Indies; it commands them all. It is of more importance to us than to any other nation."

Admiral Porter has done his work so thoroughly in this communication (of which only a small portion is given here) that little more need be said respecting the naval value of the Islands. With regard to their commercial importance, I will quote the opinion of Mr. Lyman D. Spalding, of Portsmouth, New Hampshire. He writes from personal knowledge and observation.

"The great value," says Mr. Spalding, " of St. Thomas is its harbor, which is the best in the West Indies except Havana; and for all sailing vessels it has the great advantage of being to windward; for a vessel can sail from St. Thomas to the east end of Cuba in three days; but an average passage from the east end of Cuba to St. Thomas is three weeks, as the wind blows continuously from St. Thomas to Cuba; one way a fair wind, back a head wind. This is of no moment with steamers; but bulky freight, from cheapness of transport, will generally go in sailing vessels. St. Thomas is a great distributing centre, and is the natural point of exchange for merchandise for the northern part of South America, from Trinidad to Maracaybo, the smaller windward islands, Porto Rico, and, partly so, of the east end of St. Domingo. A vessel at St. Thomas can obtain business, be at her port of discharge or loading in a few days; can buy or sell cargoes for discharge or loading at the other islands, and can obtain at St. Thomas assorted cargoes in exchange for cargoes or money carried there. It is also a money centre, and in the other islands exchange on St. Thomas is frequently quoted. It is the great repair-shop of the West Indies for vessels in distress, injured on our winter coast or on the North Atlantic, and it is very much the most valuable possession, for its size, of any of the West India Islands. Its harbor, capable of holding five hundred vessels, opens south, and, with the regular trade-winds at east, a vessel can sail in and out with a side wind, without tacking."

With regard to St. Thomas as a naval port, Mr. Spalding expresses the opinion that it is preferable to either Samana Bay or Cape St. Nicholas Mole.

"*It is ready for use,*" adds Mr. Spalding; "*it is a port and city* BUILT, *and no very large amount of money will be required to fit it for naval purposes.* But to fit Samana Bay or St. Nicholas Mole for such a use would require about as much money as the first cost of St. Thomas. It is very easy of access and departure, — one mile, and you are at sea! Whereas, Samana Bay is very long and difficult to enter or depart from by sailing vessels, and St. Nicholas Mole is also a deep inlet, with great depth of water, and its only good anchorage is at the head of the bay."

To this I could add, if necessary, other testimony of similar character.

I have had the pleasure of conversing with a distinguished officer of the Danish Navy, who now possesses a sugar-estate upon one of these islands. He is probably better acquainted with the group than any other living man, having served upon this station through all the grades of naval rank, from midshipman to admiral, from boyhood to gray hairs. For some years past he has resided in the group during most of the year, having now retired from active service. The climate, he assures me, except near the towns and coal-sheds, is as salubrious as it is delightful; for there is always a sea-breeze tempering the tropical heats, and there are no diseases which the care of man cannot as well avoid and cure as in regions supposed to be more favorable to health and longevity. With regard to the harbor of St. Thomas, he confirms the opinion of our own eminent admirals, that in time of war there is no port in the West Indies equal to it. The power holding it, he says, can strike out in every direction, and the harbor can be made as impregnable as Gibraltar.

"In fact," added he, "if the United States had all the rest of the West Indies, you would still need St. Thomas, and you would need it then more than ever."

I learn from this officer that the universal language of the group is the English, and that there is nothing in the habits or feelings of the people which is likely to prevent an easy and rapid assimilation with those of the United States. They have the free-school system as fully developed as we have, and the religion of the islands is Lutheran, rather than Calvinistic. The resident clergy have been materially assisted of late years by Moravian missionaries, and their united labors, with the influence of the schools, have done as much as could be expected towards raising the character of the colored population.

It would be easy to present to the reader a lively picture of the commercial activity of the port of St. Thomas. More than two thousand vessels enter that port sometimes in a single year, the number for 1867 being 1926. Of these, 108 were German, 427 were Danish, 628 were English, 115 were Dutch, 280 were Spanish, 92 were American, 6 were Italian, 14 were Swedish, 7 were Russian, 1 was Belgian, 38 were Venezuelian, 35 were Norwegian, 1 was Portuguese, 4 were Haytien, and 12 carried the flag of St. Domingo. The returns for last year present about the same variety and proportion. St. Thomas, in fact, being a free port, and the other good harbors of the West Indies being subjected to tariff systems more or less stringent, it has come to be, as before remarked, the great bazaar, or Stewart's store, wholesale and retail, for all that part of the world, at which firms in Birmingham, Manchester, Sheffield, Paris, Berlin, Philadelphia, Boston, and all other manufacturing centres, keep assortments of the goods which they produce.

CONCLUSION.

Here then I rest the case. The whole matter is before the reader. If he has attentively perused the foregoing pages, he knows as much of this subject as Mr. Seward or General Raasloff, and perhaps more than either of them; for, in the production of this pamphlet, I have been able to draw freely from the pigeon-holes of both, and from the excellent memory of one of them. It has been shown, I think, —

1. That we cannot repudiate Mr. Seward's bargain without

inflicting a very great and irreparable injury upon a respectable nation, our good friend and ally.

2. That, if, after paying for Alaska, we refuse to pay for these Islands, we stand dishonored before mankind, as having one rule for the strong and another for the weak.

3. That, however erroneous may be the system which permits the Executive to commit the country to purchases of land, we have no right to hold Denmark responsible for that system, nor to reform it at her expense.

4. That, when a foreign government has so much as delayed the ratification and execution of a properly concluded treaty with the United States, we have felt ourselves to be grossly wronged, and were willing to seek redress by violence.

5. That these Islands, in the opinion of professional men, have a great and peculiar value, which renders their acquisition highly desirable.

No one could have been more prejudiced against this treaty than I was. Besides having a general aversion to the acquisition of new territory, unless it lies right in the way of our inevitable march, I deemed the present a singularly unsuitable time for effecting such a purchase, or indeed any purchase that could be safely postponed. The National Debt is my religion. Having no debts of my own, it sometimes seems to me as if I owed all those billions myself, and must not spend an unnecessary dollar until we had, at least, got the debt properly funded, manageable, and in a way of being steadily reduced. We are delivered from our colossal evil, but the *bill* has not been settled; and, although I have never for an instant doubted that our great debt of honor will be paid, and paid to the satisfaction of those to whom we owe it, yet I shrink with morbid dread from any project that would add to the heavy load which the nation has to carry. It was with great pleasure that I sat last February in the gallery of the House of Representatives, and witnessed the amending of the appropriation bills, as they worked their painful way in Committee of the Whole. There was an absolute rage among members for cutting down appropriations, — which was, upon the whole, pleasing to observe, although occasionally, as it seemed, the House went too fast and too far. I listened with great satisfaction to the champions of retrenchment, Mr. Blaine, Mr. Washburne, General Butler, Mr. Scofield, General Farnsworth, and many others, and cast a silent, uncounted vote for them on almost every item.

It so happened, too, that I fell in about that time with sundry gentlemen from the West Indies, who were in Washington to ask Congress to be pleased to accept a large slice of a large Island for nothing; and when it seemed probable, in the general horror of undertaking new land, that these gentlemen might have to go home without being so much as fairly heard, I wrote a few paragraphs for the press, setting forth how much better it would be to get a large island for nothing than to buy two small ones for seven millions and a half in gold, with the privilege of taking a third island for three millions seven hundred and fifty thousand more in the same metal.

These things are proper to be mentioned here, because they show that, when the documents relating to the Danish treaty were first placed in my hands, I felt with regard to it just as seven in every ten of those who will take up this pamphlet feel. Nevertheless, being moved thereto by gentlemen deeply interested in the subject, in and out of Congress, Americans and Danes, I examined those papers, and discovered that I had been opposed to the ratification of the treaty without knowing anything about it. It seemed to me, also, that there was in these documents the material for an interesting story, which, being simply told, would certainly throw light upon the art and mystery of diplomacy, and perhaps assist to prevent our doing a cruel wrong to a friendly power, respectable in every thing but size.

Alaska, I repeat, has been paid for. It remains to be seen whether we really have one rule in dealing with a strong nation, and another in dealing with a weak one. We are to show, perhaps, by our conduct in this case, whether we are, or are not, the kind of people who can truckle to a giant and trample on a child.

APPENDIX.

APPENDIX.

I AM enabled to lay before the reader a valuable communication made recently to the Honorable Chairman of the Senate Committee on Foreign Relations, by Captain G. V. Fox, who served his country with so much ability and distinction during the war as Assistant Secretary of the Navy.

CAPTAIN FOX TO THE HONORABLE CHARLES SUMNER.

BOSTON, MASS., February 27, 1869.

HON. CHARLES SUMNER, *United States Senator, Chairman Senate Committee of Foreign Relations, Washington, D. C.*

SIR:—I have the honor to acknowledge the receipt of your letter of the 19th instant, requesting my opinion of the value of the island of St. Thomas.

Having spent several years amongst the West India Islands, on board naval and commercial vessels, I am somewhat familiar with those localities. St. Thomas is a small island situated sixteen hundred miles south southeast of New York. It contains about two thirds of the area of the present District of Columbia, and resembles it in being broken up into heights susceptible of easy defence. The harbor is one of the best in the West Indies, admirable for naval purposes, and fully equal to all the requirements of the commerce of those seas.

Besides possessing a sufficient depth of water, and an extensive area, for the accommodation of fleets, transports, and convoys, it has natural advantages for defence, seldom found in connection with the harbors of the West Indies.

The entrance is narrow, and capable of being obstructed; the hills on both sides have a commanding elevation, sufficient to place the batteries thereon above the reach of ships' guns, whilst an attacking fleet would be subjected to their plunging fire. The harbor on the land side is covered by similar eminences. These are conditions which, together with its small area and insular position, give satisfactory security for a naval depot.

The eminent geographical, strategic, and commercial position which St. Thomas occupies arrests the attention of the most casual observer of the world's chart. It is the apex of the West Indies; opposite is the continent of Africa, equidistant are the eastern shores of North and South America; on one side is Western Europe, and on the other the route to India and the Pacific; in the rear are the Spanish Main, Central America, the West Indies, Mexico, and those two great internal bodies of salt water belonging to this continent, the Caribbean Sea and the Gulf of Mexico.

It is on the route of our trade with the West Indies, Brazil, the coasts of Africa, and the countries lying beyond the Cape of Good Hope and Cape Horn. Vessels from England and Western Europe stop there on their way to the tropical countries of this hemisphere, the west coasts of America, and Australia. It has gradually come to be the commercial centre of the West Indies, and the distributing depot as well as the coaling and repair station of a tonnage greater than that of Boston and Baltimore combined; thus demonstrating that its advantages have commanded the approval of practical merchants. When the Isthmus of Darien shall be cut through by a ship canal, its importance will be enhanced. That event depends on like economic calculations with the Suez Canal, now being opened. Trade which has been forced to use the routes around Cape Horn and the Cape of Good Hope will seek these artificial channels, and the base of naval operations must be in their vicinity. The lines of communication between this country and all others cross the ocean. The central position of the United States, its vast shore line, prodigious resources, and the instincts of its people, point to a maritime supremacy. The distribution and exchange of the multiplying products of the earth are becoming every day more dependent upon coal, inexhaustible quantities of which abound in the United States.

Before the application of steam to naval purposes, sea-going vessels were built of wood where ship-timber and cheap labor were abundant. Relying upon the winds alone for propulsion, they performed the longest voyages without entering port. Now, naval vessels and the principal commercial ships are steamers, constructed with skilled labor found near manufacturing centres. A large portion of their internal space is occupied with machinery and coal, leaving a limited part for cargo, supplies, and munitions.

Every few thousand miles they must enter port for coal and repairs; hence their movements are limited to passages from one coaling-port to another. These altered conditions impose upon commercial countries the establishment of coaling and repair stations along ocean lines, just as they are found necessary upon our great railroad routes.

The blockade of the Southern coast, equal in extent to the Atlantic border of Europe, was maintained, owing to the introduction of steam for naval uses, and the immediate capture from the Rebels of carefully selected stations for coaling and repairing our fleets. A blockading force of steamers cannot be driven from its station by bad weather, as was the case formerly with sailing squadrons.

Nearly one half of all the steamers engaged in this severe duty were constantly under repair, and the adjacent ports, which foresight had provided, furnished, therefore, the base essential for naval success.

If we had been defeated in our attempts to secure these places, the blockade could not have been sustained, and the casualties of battle would have been irreparable.

England menaces our coast with four strategic points, — Halifax, Bermuda, Nassau, and Jamaica. At these stations were concentrated the munitions and supplies which encouraged the Rebels, and afforded to them material aid. Owing to their proximity, British merchants were enabled to use for blockade purposes small light-draft steamers, well adapted for entering the numerous shallow harbors of the South at night. If these positions had belonged to the United States, or if there had been no English stations so close to us, larger steamers would have been necessary to attempt the blockade; such vessels must have had a greater draft of water, thereby restricting their entrance to daylight and fewer ports.

That I do not exaggerate the importance of the naval stations of Great Britain on the coast of the United States is evident in remembering that, of fifteen hundred vessels and $32,000,000 of property condemned prize to the Navy, nearly all belonged to British merchants, and was captured passing between the English ports I have mentioned and our Southern harbors. Excepting a naval force upon our rivers, and co-operating movements with the army, the Navy of the United States, during the Rebellion, was shedding its blood and expending the treasure of the country in efforts defensive against Great Britain. That power possesses at convenient intervals, along the routes of our trade, all around the earth, ports for coaling and repairing vessels.

No other country, excepting the United States, has coal for exportation; and since we own no stations abroad, and were not permitted, during the late war, to land coal on foreign territory for the use of our navy, we became entirely dependent upon England for means to reach the seas where American commerce was being pillaged. The naval experience of the Rebellion teaches that *in future wars steam power only can be used successfully against an enemy's commerce.* Therefore the nation having naval depots and surplus coal will occupy a commanding position in a maritime struggle.

Steamers for the destruction of merchant vessels may, possibly, be "improvised," but coaling-stations are only acquired by purchase or bloodshed.

At the commencement of our struggle, the South had neither ports, cruisers, coal, munitions, nor sailors. All her resources for successful plunder of our commerce flowed from illegal expeditions, which left the shores of England by connivance of her Government, and subsequently found coal and refitment at her depot stations. Experience shows that *the successful pursuit of hostile steamers cannot be maintained without having coaling-stations where neutral restrictions do not exist.*

The persistent unfriendliness of the British Government made a painful impression upon Mr. Lincoln, and led him to reflect on the best means of lifting his country from humiliating dependence upon foreign governments for naval repairs and supplies of coal during war. Hence his authority for commencing negotiations looking to the purchase of St. Thomas.

His attention was early attracted to this island by its superior position, the fitness of its harbor, the appliances already there for naval and commercial uses, and its pre-eminence over all other ports mentioned in capabilities of defence and freedom from the expense and entanglements of large territorial acquisitions. The value was measured approximately by remembering the cost of our efforts in obtaining coaling-stations on the Southern coast, and reflecting upon the immense value of the menacing points belonging to Great Britain, near us.

The experience of centuries has demonstrated that defensible depot-stations in waters where a fleet is intended to act are invaluable for the protection they afford to commerce, the efficiency they give to naval power, and the economy they produce in repairing and supplying such force. History is full of the struggles of nations for the control of such positions; Rhodes, Malta, Minorca, Gibraltar, Louisburg, Havana, and Carthagena readily occur to the memory. Their loss was followed by diminished naval power; their gain, by enlarged influence.

Now, when coal has superseded sails for war purposes, and is increasing rapidly for commercial uses, *the old reasons for their establishment have become imperative.* The winds are everywhere, but steamers depend upon coaling-ports for their continuous efficiency. My judgment earnestly approved of this effort to acquire St. Thomas for a naval station.

The reasons which made it wise and patriotic for Mr. Lincoln to open negotiations to this end have lost none of their

Appendix.

New grounds for favoring the object come con-
...to notice, and our country can hardly fulfil the great
...s expected of her, unless she secures, when the opportu-
... is presented, a position which by strategic art will serve
... an outwork to the coast of our Union, and give additional
efficiency to the means of defending our commerce and our
Atlantic and Pacific communications.

    With great respect,
     Your obedient servant,
(Signed,)   G. V. FOX.

www.ingramcontent.com/pod-product-compliance
Lightning Source LLC
Chambersburg PA
CBHW020338090426
42735CB00009B/1583